Gnostic Writings
on the Soul

Books in the
SkyLight Illuminations Series

Gnostic Writings on the Soul

Annotated & Explained

Translation & Annotation
by Andrew Phillip Smith

Foreword by Stephan A. Hoeller

Walking Together, Finding the Way ®
SKYLIGHT PATHS®
PUBLISHING
Woodstock, Vermont

Gnostic Writings on the Soul:
Annotated & Explained

2007 First Printing
Translation, annotation, and introductory material © 2007 by Andrew Phillip Smith
Foreword © 2007 by Stephan A. Hoeller

Library of Congress Cataloging-in-Publication Data

Smith, Andrew Phillip, 1966–
Gnostic writings on the soul : annotated & explained / translations and annotations by Andrew Phillip Smith.
    p. cm.
Includes bibliographical references.
ISBN-13: 978-1-59473-220-1 (quality pbk.)
ISBN-10: 1-59473-220-5 (quality pbk.)
1. Exegesis on the soul. 2. Hymn of the soul. 3. Gnosticism. I. Exegesis on the soul. 2007. II. Hymn of the pearl. 2007. III. Title.
BT1392.E932S65 2007
299'.932—dc22

                                                                    2006037624

10 9 8 7 6 5 4 3 2 1

Manufactured in the United States of America
Cover design: Walter C. Bumford III
Cover art: Plate 24, *The First Book of Urizen* copy A, William Blake (1794).

> SkyLight Paths Publishing is creating a place where people of different spiritual traditions come together for challenge and inspiration, a place where we can help each other understand the mystery that lies at the heart of our existence.
>
> SkyLight Paths sees both believers and seekers as a community that increasingly transcends traditional boundaries of religion and denomination—people wanting to learn from each other, *walking together, finding the way*.

SkyLight Paths, "Walking Together, Finding the Way" and colophon are trademarks of LongHill Partners, Inc., registered in the U.S. Patent and Trademark Office.

Walking Together, Finding the Way®
Published by SkyLight Paths® Publishing
A Division of LongHill Partners, Inc.
Sunset Farm Offices, Route 4, P.O. Box 237
Woodstock, VT 05091
Tel: (802) 457-4000   Fax: (802) 457-4004
www.skylightpaths.com

For my soul and my spirit.

Contents ☐

Foreword □

Stephan A. Hoeller

This book has as its subject two Gnostic myths. The use of myths in the Gnostic tradition is well known, although the nature and purpose of such myths is not always understood. In his work *Essays on a Science of Mythology* (written in collaboration with Carl G. Jung), the great Hungarian mythologist Carl Kerenyi wrote that "the Gnostics can tell us about what comes closest to mythology in mysticism." The mystical mythology of the Gnostics is thus a phenomenon of unique character and distinction. Unlike the mythologies of many peoples, including the Homeric Greeks, the Gnostic myths were rooted in highly charged personal experience of exalted states of consciousness. At the heart of Gnosticism lies the experience of Gnosis, which has been understood by several present-day scholars as being the experience of the ontological self. This self (recognized by the Gnostics as the *pneuma*, or spirit) was regarded as being of the same nature as God, so that such experience would inevitably join human consciousness with divinity. In *The Gnostic Gospels*, Elaine Pagels aptly characterized the personal mystical experience of the Gnostics as "Self-Knowledge as Knowledge of God." This is the knowledge that is then turned by Gnostics into that most creative of symbolic communications known as myth.

Already in classical antiquity, the Greek word *mythos* had come to mean a tale of a nonhistorical nature with protagonists of a supernatural sort, such as gods, goddesses, heroes, and unearthly creatures. The eighteenth- and nineteenth-century Romantics used the word *myth* to describe a story possessing a timeless character and dealing with transmundane concerns. Most definitions suggest that a myth is an account that is not historically true, yet represents an expression of timeless truths. Mythic events occur not in ordinary time but once upon a time, in an unspecified time similar to what the Australian aboriginals have called "dreamtime." Gnostic mythmakers drew their inspiration from such timeless experiences. Most important, their exalted experiences of Gnosis could not be expressed just as well in a prosaic way, for such experiences could be brought to consciousness best in the form of myth. Hence, the overwhelming majority of Gnostic scriptures are mythic rather than factual in character, for myths constitute the optimal instrumentalities whereby the insights glimpsed by the Gnostic sages were made available to their fellow seekers after Gnosis.

The study of Gnostic scriptures discloses four principal mythologems, which appear and reappear with great frequency in such literature. Some scriptures are predominantly devoted to one or the other of these themes, while in other instances one finds them in various combinations. These four themes are as follows: (1) the myth of the feminine deific principle (frequently called Sophia); (2) the myth of the imperfect demiurge (intermediate creator) of the world; (3) the myth of the Redeemer (usually identified with Jesus) who redeems souls not from sin but from terrestrial confinement; and lastly (4) the myth of the soul's journey from its original heavenly habitat, its capture by dark forces of unconsciousness and imprisonment in matter, and its glorious return to the blissful light-world after its liberation.

The two scriptures translated and annotated by Andrew Phillip Smith belong obviously to this fourth category. *The Exegesis on the Soul* is part of the well-known collection of scriptures usually known as the Nag Hammadi Library. This scripture could have accurately been titled *The Journey of the Soul* instead, for it describes in poetic narrative form the origins, descent, and liberated ascent of a being called Psyche (Soul). It has been suggested by some scholars that the author of this scripture may have been a woman, for the existential condition of the female sex is expressed by the author with such conviction that one suspects the hand of experience. *The Exegesis on the Soul* and the second mythic poem included in this work, *The Hymn of the Pearl*, describe in mythic metaphors the great story that is implicit in all Gnostic writings, although it appears in explicit form in others. This story may be briefly summarized thus:

In a time before time there was no person or thing, only an all-encompassing unitary essence of light. From this boundless and luminous unity there came forth individual sparks of light, which eventually came to be confined in shells of profound darkness. In these prisons the sparks fell into an uneasy state of sleep from which only the experience of transcendental knowing (Gnosis) could awaken them. Such Gnosis has the power to release the spark from the prison of its earthly embodiment and allows it to return to its original home, the supernal realm of light and freedom.

While contemporary modern and postmodern thought in its materialistic alienation from transcendence is unwilling to appreciate it, the liberation and ascension of the soul-spark are not accomplished without help from outside. This help is provided by the Messenger who comes from the supernal light world in order to facilitate the awakening and liberation of the souls. This is the core-myth, the essential story that is told and retold in many myths, but that also is present in a particularly pure and clear form in the two mystic poems of this work. Both myths are tales of "the hero's journey," to apply a phrase popularized by Joseph Campbell. In one of the tales the hero is female, in the other he is presumed to be male. The Messenger bears the title of "Bridegroom" in the first, while in the second, the messengership is represented by a magic letter written by the Powers of Light, a letter that flies on the wings of an eagle and speaks with a powerful voice.

There is no doubt that the Gnostic writers applied the symbolism of the spark of light to the human soul (or spirit). The human being was understood to consist of an outer, personal selfhood and an inner, spiritual self. Knowledge of the interior spark is withheld from the outer human by the very existential human condition itself, inasmuch as ignorance of spiritual realities is a hallmark of earthly existence. The transcendent God is unknown in this world and this fateful ignorance can only be disspelled by revelation. To the Gnostic, revelation is not like the Torah, Qur'an, or even the New Testament. What is revealed is spiritual, liberating knowledge in lieu of doctrine and commandment. What saves is neither faith nor works, but Gnosis. Believing in the death and resurrection of Jesus and associated teachings will not liberate the soul, but Gnosis will.

As can be seen from either or both of the scriptures here under consideration, the central turning point of this entire picture is the experience of Gnosis. Once the Bridegroom brings the means of awakening to the grieving soul of *The Exegesis on the Soul*, and once the traveller in Egypt reads the awakening letter in *The Hymn of the Pearl*, liberating Gnosis has arrived, and all is well.

Today there can be little doubt that in the Christian communities in the first three or even four centuries C.E. there lived many persons who strove for salvific Gnosis. There is no valid reason why these good people and their inspiring scriptures should be denied the name "Gnostic." There was a time when that term tended to raise many eyebrows. The reason for such attitudes was to be found in some writings of heresy-hunting Church Fathers in the early centuries. These persons were primarily churchly politicians who, in the manner of politicians in every age, were intent on blackening the reputation of their rivals. Today we find that the scriptures used by these alleged heretics show no sign of mental imbalance or antisocial behavior. Gnostics they were, and usually they called themselves by that name, as well as by the name Christian. Today we have discovered a historical basis for the word *Gnostic* as a valid term of definition and self-definition. More perhaps than other scriptures of Gnostic derivation, the two mythic poems here translated and annotated depict the experiential dimensions of Gnosticism. Here we see the alienation, degradation, and abuse of our souls graphically depicted. Here we also see the coming of the awakening Helper, and the glorious ascent of these same souls to their original home, the world of light and fullness. Scriptures of this kinds were always the agents of awakening and Gnosis, and we may be assured that they can play the same role today. Andrew Phillip Smith and SkyLight Paths are to be thanked for presenting us with this volume!

Introduction ☐

Do you have a soul? If so, how do you know this? Is the soul your inner life, the sum of whatever you are thinking and feeling? Is your soul imprisoned in your body, or do body and soul coexist in a happy union? Is your soul immortal? Does your soul come from the heavens? Does it long to return to the Divine, or is it immersed in the distractions of everyday life?

The concept of the soul appears in almost every human society, at every age in history. There are many variations of the idea, but certain themes persist, and the concept of the soul is part of the heritage of humanity. We will be focusing on the Gnostic view of the soul, which developed between the first and third centuries. There were a variety of Gnostic sects during this time. They had a wide range of beliefs, but they all believed that mankind was in a fallen state, and yet that it was possible for individuals to attain direct knowledge of God and a higher reality, and they used myth and metaphor to convey the situation of mankind. Most Gnostics were Christian, but they were regarded as heretics by the church fathers, and the triumph of orthodoxy in the early church marginalized the Gnostics. Two ancient allegorical tales, *The Exegesis on the Soul* and *The Hymn of the Pearl*, follow the trials and triumphs of the soul, and are tales of a fall and redemption. But the advanced ideas concerning the soul that were used by the Gnostics did not appear from a vacuum, nor did they simply die out when Gnostic groups disappeared. They take their place in a continuum of soul concepts that run from prehistory to the present day. The Gnostic view of the soul is particularly inclusive, and the Gnostics creatively drew from Jewish, Greek, and Christian traditions.

When we use the word *soul* in our contemporary Western, English-speaking culture, what do we mean? The term often refers to the presence or absence of a certain quality of genuineness. We might say that a particularly cold-blooded coworker, who is unfriendly and does everything by the book, has no soul. Or that a bland, newly built city suburb, filled with fast-food outlets and chain stores, has no soul. Clearly, there is an aspect of individuality involved here—something that is mass-produced may be said to have no soul. The words *heart* and *soul* are often used together, and they may indeed be synonymous. Where one's heart is, there one's soul is also.

Soul may also refer to the essential nature of something—we might refer to "the soul of popular culture" or say that moderate Muslims are fighting with extremist Muslims for "the soul of Islam."

Other cultures and eras have not been so vague about the soul. Among the vast range of ideas, we can distinguish three broad categories of soul that appear in various forms across time and traditions. The first, and the most primitive, is the notion of the soul as the vital force that animates the body. This is the soul associated with bodily functions such as the breath, or even with the body's shadow. The second is the soul as the inner world, the stream of consciousness, our subjective feelings of ourselves, our sense perceptions, our thoughts, emotions, and desires. This is the meaning of soul in modern psychology and science. Finally, there is the soul as a divine and immortal entity that is closely connected to God or to the highest spiritual level of the universe. (I will generally use the word *spirit* for this variety of soul, because it is the term used by the Gnostics.) The Gnostics tied a number of these ideas together. They felt that the soul that was concerned only with the body and the outside world of matter was a fallen soul, but it could return to its source by seeking the Divine. According to the Gnostics, humans had individual souls and an element of the divine spirit.

The Vital Force
The most basic conception of the soul treats it simply as the life principle—a living body has a soul, but a dead body has none. Simple observation

shows us that there is an empirical difference between a living body and a dead body. A living body is warm, it moves, and it breathes. A dead body does none of these things. It would seem that breath is the most fundamental indication that a body is alive (witness the holding of a mirror to the mouth to see whether the breath clouds the mirror, a convention familiar from many murder mysteries). The word for soul or spirit in many languages is either the same as, or etymologically connected to, the word for breath. For example, the Hebrew *ruach*, Greek *pneuma* and *psyche*, Arabic *ruh*, Latin *spiritus*, and a word in the language of the Ewe people of Togo all mean both "breath" and "soul" or "spirit." When the last breath leaves the body and the person dies, is there something more than the content of the lungs that is departing? Perhaps it was from such an observation that the most primitive and simple notion of the soul was born. The connection between breath and spirit has even survived in English, and the English word *spirit* and words connected with breathing, such as *respiration*, come from the Latin *spiritus*, which means both "breath" and "spirit."

The Inner World

In modern English, the terms *soul* and *spirit* are often used more or less interchangeably, but in some ancient cultures they were distinct entities. In Gnosticism particularly, the soul was one's inner life, while the spirit was divine in origin.[1] The inner life is that world of sensation, feeling, thought, decision, attraction, and reaction that only we are privy to. Regardless of whether this inner world lies unexamined or whether we have some knowledge of it through psychology or a spiritual discipline, or through some intuitive self-knowledge, we each have an inner world. The quality of this inner world can vary considerably from person to person, or indeed from moment to moment in the same person. The inner life of a murderer is of a different quality to the inner life of a well-adjusted parent, which is of a different quality to the inner life of a saint.

The Spirit

But what of the transcendent aspect of the soul—the immortal, divine part of ourselves? The Gnostics referred to this as spirit, and differentiated it from the personal soul. Indeed, it is only the crudest forms of religion and spirituality that imagine that our individual personalities, with all of their contradictions and mundane concerns, can become immortal. The soul as the inner world is the ultimate in subjectivity, but the spirit is generally seen as something that, while it may be experienced personally, has a universal quality. This is the divine self, which maintains its connection with God, and is not concerned with food, money, shelter or the desire for a mate. The experience of the spirit is still an internal one, of course, but is not typically part of everyone's day-to-day experience, and is generally thought to be available only to those who hold to a religion or who practice spiritual disciplines.

The Gnostic Soul

To the Gnostics, the soul was an intermediate level of existence. Gnostics had a threefold division of the human: body or matter, soul, and spirit. Spirit was divine and was also referred to as the Holy Spirit, as in Christianity. In Gnosticism, the soul in its undeveloped state is nothing special; everyone has one, and the usual state of the soul is described in *The Exegesis on the Soul* as a prostitute, selling herself to a multitude of worthless men who are lowlifes, thieves, and adulterers.

But the soul was not always like this. The soul has fallen. Once, the soul lived in the divine realm and was united with the spirit. According to one view, which is expressed in *The Hymn of the Pearl*, the soul is a prince sent on a mission, and the spirit is his older brother. But the prince becomes entangled in the material world and forgets his mission. A letter from his parents in his home kingdom reminds him of his task and he succeeds in his mission. He then returns to his former splendor, but with a greater maturity.

From the point of view in *The Exegesis on the Soul*, however, the soul has fallen into prostitution and has been seduced by the material world.

The soul in *The Exegesis* is not on a mission, but by the end of her story she has also matured, and instead of the androgynous virgin that she was when the story opened, she has become a bride.

The Gnostics, who flourished in the second and third centuries C.E., had some of the most developed concepts concerning the soul. They began to decline in numbers and in influence during the third century. Various forms of Gnosticism survived in small pockets here and there for several centuries, but its subsequent influence on mainstream Christianity was minimal. The Gnostics did not write philosophical texts or construct dogma; instead, they used a variety of less direct methods—myth, metaphor, symbolism, and the esoteric interpretation of scripture to express their understandings.

The two pieces of Gnostic writings presented in this book—*The Exegesis on the Soul* and *The Hymn of the Pearl*—represent some typically Gnostic modes of writing. *The Exegesis* gives us a myth of the downfall and redemption of the soul—which, in this case, is a female figure. Besides the story itself, *The Exegesis* also provides us with a direct interpretation of the story, along with excerpts from Hebrew and Christian scripture and Homer's *Odyssey*, which are also used to illustrate the plight of the soul. *The Hymn of the Pearl* also gives us a tale of exile and return, but gives us only the slightest key to its interpretation. It is an intimate first-person narrative.

We will return to the Gnostics later. Their ideas about the soul and the spirit did not exist in isolation—all religions and cultures have had some conception of the soul. In the Gnostic conception we may perceive Gnosticism's dual inheritance of the fundamental Jewish view of the soul, in which the importance of the soul is in its relationship with God, and the Platonic concept of the soul that is imprisoned in the body. Orthodox Christianity clashed with Gnosticism and the church fathers read Gnostic texts in order to refute them. This led indirectly to Christianity absorbing a certain amount of influence from Gnosticism. Gnosticism went into decline from the third century C.E., but Gnostic ideas survived in the

Manichaean religion. This vanished religion was once widespread, and evidence of Manichaeanism has been found as far west as Spain and as far east as China. It was founded by Mani, a teacher who was born in the Persian Empire in the third century c.e.

Other religions, such as Islam, Hinduism, and Buddhism, have their own developed notions of the soul, and the idea has persisted, however weakly, in Western secular culture, despite its taking a battering from the mechanistic conception of humanity and the universe. I have noted that the general conception of soul in modern secular society is somewhat vague. In the world's religions, in esoteric spiritual thought, and in new religious movements, the idea of the soul is more distinct, but the core concepts of these traditions are often inaccessible to outsiders. The historical study of these and vanished traditions can help us understand the nature of the soul. What follows constitutes a brief history of the soul.

Primitive Notions of the Soul

Humanity's very first understandings of the existence of the soul and its nature are lost in time, as is any knowledge of the individuals or cultures that were responsible for it. Probably it was an idea that formed independently in many places at many times. Though the earliest conceptions of the soul are lost to us, we can still examine the ideas held by so-called primitive societies. James Frazer, the author of the seminal work *The Golden Bough*, describes how a nineteenth-century European Christian missionary rather condescendingly told a group of "Australian blacks" (Frazer's term): "I am not one, as you think, but two." Upon hearing this, they laughed. "You may laugh as much as you like," continued the missionary. "I tell you that I am two in one; this great body that you see is one; within that there is another little one which is not visible. The great body dies, and is buried, but the little body flies away when the great one dies." To the missionary's surprise, one of the Aborigines replied, "Yes, yes. We also are two, we also have a little body within the breast."[2]

All primitive peoples seem to have some idea of the soul. The range of ideas is not uniform, and they cannot be guaranteed to be in any way identical or similar to ancient beliefs, but they are worth an exploration.

In primitive religion, the soul is often conceived of as being connected to a part of the body. The soul, or a particular aspect of it, is located in the brain, or in the heart. Or the soul may be understood as being something separate from the physical body but related to it, as in a person's shadow or reflection, or in an animal that is somehow connected to the person. These concepts are referred to as the "external soul" by anthropologists. These are truly primitive concepts, indicating that the primitive person is unable to conceive of himself without reference to something external, is unable to look within himself, unable to understand his internal world, unable to know himself. The well-known superstition that one's soul can be taken away by a camera is a continuing remnant of these beliefs.

Many examples have been recorded since the nineteenth century. The people of Bank's Islands in Vanuata, Oceania, expect death if they see their own reflections in a cave pool, presumably thinking that this is a sign that the soul has already left the body (in many cultures, the soul can vacate the body weeks, even years, before death). The soul is sometimes thought to have left the body during dreams. Shadows are also seen to be an external soul, and even the ancient Egyptians held the shadow to be an independent element of the human being. The name of an individual, too, was sacred to the Egyptians, as well as to recent primitive cultures, and in some way is felt to represent the essence of an individual, and thus an external soul.

The soul may be connected to certain bodily functions and excreta or bodily fluids. Blood (menstrual or internal), semen, sweat, tears, and saliva can all be seen to be an expression of the soul, along with hair, nails, and skin flakings. These are obviously associated with the soul as a basic, animating force. Hair and nails continue to grow after death and may therefore be connected with survival after death. Modern occult traditions also place magical importance on these bodily products, as well as on the soul being able to leave the body during sleep or illness.

Thus, souls can be in exile from their bodies, and bodies can become soulless shells, or can lack souls even if the original personality is retained. Souls can leave the human and inhabit animals, and, vice versa, animal souls can inhabit human bodies. The soul of a witch or sorcerer can move into another human in addition to the original soul.

The fear of seeing one's reflection in water, which is attested in a variety of primitive societies, is in distinct contrast to the positive use of the image of the mirror in *The Hymn of the Pearl* and other Gnostic and early Christian literature, where the mirror is a metaphor for seeing oneself objectively and the joy this brings. It will be obvious that there is little that is spiritually transcendent in these possibilities. For the most part, they are governed by fear or by the wish for power over others.

But there are more sophisticated concepts even within primitive societies, ones that resemble the developed concepts of the great religions and philosophies. The Mbua people of Rio Branco in Brazil assert that each person has three souls: a good soul, a bad soul, and a third protective soul that guards and observes. Australian Aborigines consider themselves to have a real soul, which pre-exists the birth of the physical body and survives death, plus a trickster soul, which can leave the body and inhabit other bodies.

The *Ka*, the *Ba*, and the Egyptian Soul

Let us turn our attention to humanity's most ancient civilizations. The ancient Mesopotamian cultures of Sumeria, Akkadia, and Babylonia give us little direct information regarding the soul. In the surviving texts, there is an existence after death, which is a bleak affair, an unhappy, shadowy continuance of this life in a dry, dusty, and barren underworld. Although the ancient *Epic of Gilgamesh*, in which Gilgamesh tries to attain immortality after his best friend Enkidu is killed by the gods, might be seen as a story of the soul's journey, there are few direct mentions of the soul in the text—Gilgamesh's friend Enkidu is referred to as "my second soul," and Gilgamesh meets a woman whose drinks refresh the soul. Beyond this, the surviving texts offer us little.

It is in Egyptian civilization that we first discover a number of highly developed concepts relating to the soul. The ancient Egyptians, like some of the primitive beliefs that we have mentioned, and like the Gnostics, thought that each person had more than one soul, or more than one internal element. The Egyptian beliefs are never clearly defined in the surviving texts, but Egyptologists have tried to work out the underlying concepts from their contexts. The most common Egyptian terms that correspond to a soul are the *ka*, the *ba*, and the *akh* (or *khu* or *akkhu*). *Ka* is often translated as "life force" or "vital force." The *ka* is what makes a human, or even a god, alive. *Ka* is transmitted from one being to another, from parents to children. The being Atum embraced Shu and Tefnut, the first gods, and transmitted his *ka* to them. There were also different levels of *ka*. The *ka* of a god was of a different order than a human *ka*, and the *ka* of a pharaoh was of a very different quality than the *ka* of an ordinary Egyptian; for god, pharaoh, and commoner, the possession of *ka* was essential for existence. When the body died, the *ka* usually survived, and a synonym for death was "going to one's *ka*." But after death, the *ka* was still not entirely independent of the body, and the survival of the *ka* depended on the Egyptian funerary rites being correctly held, and on the continuing survival of the mummified body. If these conditions were not fulfilled, it seems that the *ka* simply ceased to exist. After death, the *ka* remained close to the tomb and was thought to feed on the offerings, and even on the images of food and drink that decorated the sepulcher. The idea of leaving food for the departed soul seems strange to us now, but we might ask ourselves what exactly we are doing when we leave flowers at the graveside. All of this would suggest that the *ka* resembled primitive notions of soul as an animating principle, intimately connected to the body and matter. (The relationship between the body and the soul has long been a contentious issue.) The ancient Egyptians can probably be considered the first civilization to assert the immortality of the soul, or at least its existence after death. Still, there does not seem to have been any association between the *ka* and the internal life of a human being.

The *ba* is a more sophisticated belief, a more spiritualized concept, yet a more evasive idea than the *ka*. *Ba* is often translated as "soul." In the Old Kingdom, it referred to the manifestation of a god. Its hieroglyph was a human-headed bird, and it was often represented pictorially in papyrus texts and wall paintings as such. The role of the *ba* during life is not described in our sources, but after death it somehow represented the individual person. Correspondingly, the *ba* of a god represented the character of that god: the *ba* of Re was the phoenix (also the ram), the *ba* of Horus the hawk, and so on.

The *akh* may reasonably be rendered as spirit, though it may also appear in translation as the "soul" or "transfigured spirit." "The *akh* belongs to heaven, the corpse to earth."³ In the *akh*, we perhaps have the first example of what the Gnostics called the spirit, an element of the human that transcends ordinary experience, which is glorious, shining, and belongs to the celestial realm. The development of this idea through the history of Egypt suggests that initially only pharaohs were thought to have an *akh*. *Akh* resembles later ideas of spirit more than *ka* or *ba* resemble later concepts of soul. But in these three terms, the *ka*, the *ba*, and the *akh*, we may see the initial outline of three broad conceptions of the soul explained earlier: the soul as life force, the soul as something that is not the body but is still distinctively that person, and the soul as a transcendent principle that connects humanity with the gods, with heaven, and with the stars.

Ancient Egyptian civilization lasted for over three and a half millennia, and it is unreasonable to suppose that concepts remained rigidly defined during that entire period of time. There were also other non-corporeal elements that made up the human being, and these seem to have coexisted with the ideas of the *ka*, *ba*, and *akh*. The name and the shadow have already been mentioned with reference to primitive societies. Like the *akh*, the *sahu* also referred to the spirit, while the *ab* referred to the heart (in the emotional sense). The *ab* survived death only to be weighed by Thoth and Anubis on a gigantic scale. On the other end of the balance was placed a feather—a symbol not only of lightness but also of flight. A crocodile waited below to devour the hearts that were heavier than a feather, and Osiris sat above the scales, perhaps waiting to receive the hearts that passed the test.

The Soul in the Hebrew Bible

The pivotal point in the early history of the Jewish people was the exodus from Egypt. This gives us, if I may pun slightly, a point of departure to examine the concept of the soul in ancient Judaism. Egyptian ideas about the soul do not have a very direct connection to our modern thought, though they may have influenced Greek thought early on (witness Plato's story of his ancestor Solon meeting Egyptian priests) and been influential during the Hellenistic period. But the ancient Jewish conception of the soul has survived into modern Judaism, and has begotten Christianity and directly influenced Islam. We may say quite reasonably that the subsequent development of the idea of the soul in the West owes equally to Judaism and to Greek thought.

Two words in the Hebrew Bible are most commonly translated as "soul" or "spirit"—*nefesh* and *ruach*—and a third, *lev*, refers to the heart and is translated as such, but also carries the meaning of consciousness or conscience. *Nefesh* runs a gamut of meaning from the physical to the abstract. In its most primitive meaning, it refers to the throat, just as does the Greek *thumos*, which also has a similar range of meanings. Beyond the meaning of throat, and its connection with taking in food and drink and breath, *nefesh* refers to the animating life force, much as did the *ka* in Egypt. But in the later books of the Hebrew Bible it came to mean the individual self, often the entire person, and can be a roundabout way of saying "I" or "me." The word translated as "soul" is usually *nefesh*. The Hebrew Bible is concerned with the relationship between humanity in general, specifically with the Jewish people and God. The importance of the soul is that it wishes to know God and longs for God—this is the great contribution of the Jewish approach to the soul. The relationship between the soul and God is most beautifully expressed in these psalms: "My soul thirsts for God, for the living God. When shall I come and behold the face of God?" (Psalm 42:2) and "For God alone my soul waits in silence, for my hope is from Him" (Psalm 62:5). In the psalms, the soul may be joined to the dust and earth, but it longs for God; it may be troubled, embittered, or sorrowful, but the presence of God can make it joyful and quiet.

The Hebrew word *ruach* is usually rendered in English as "spirit," and, in distinction from the *nefesh*, which longs for God, the *ruach*, to some extent, partakes of the nature of God. As Ecclesiastes 12:7, says "The dust returns to the earth as it was, and the spirit returns to God who gave it." *Ruach* also means "wind," and by studying its usage in the different sections of the Hebrew Bible, scholars have found that the word *ruach* progressed from having a concrete, natural meaning of wind, to meaning breath or one who breathes, and finally to a spiritualized notion of spirit.

Ancient Greek Ideas about the Soul

The works of Homer are among the oldest literature in Greek. *The Iliad* and *The Odyssey* are thought to have been put together in the eighth century B.C.E. Homer is a shadowy figure. He is popularly known as a blind poet, but even the smallest details of his life are disputed, and the Homeric epics may be considered to be more the result of a long period of oral tradition than the works of an individual. In Homer, the soul is a property of living people and is always mentioned in connection with death or battle, which suggests that the soul was understood primarily as being the vital force. When someone dies, the soul goes down to the underworld where it has a bleak shadelike existence similar to that of the Mesopotamian underworld or the Jewish Sheol. However, down the ages, Odysseus's trials and wanderings found in *The Odyssey* have been interpreted as allegorically representing the journey of the soul. An otherwise unknown first-century B.C.E. writer named Heraclitus wrote a work entitled *The Homeric Allegories*, and the neo-Platonists Plotinus and Porphyry also attempted to interpret Homer allegorically. Certainly, *The Odyssey* lends itself easily to this kind of interpretation, and there have been modern attempts to perceive *The Odyssey* as the story of the soul's journey.

By the fifth and sixth centuries B.C.E., the Greeks believed that all living creatures, including animals, possessed souls. The doctrine of Pythagoras (c. 582–c. 507 B.C.E.) was particularly concerned with metempsychosis, the transmigration of souls. This well-known version of reincarnation allowed for the survival of the soul after death. The surviving soul could take on another body, and people and animals alike took part in the transmigration. Socrates' friend Xenophanes mentioned a story about Pythagoras:[4] "Once, they say, he was passing by when a puppy was being whipped, and he took pity and said: 'Stop, do not beat it; it is the soul of a friend that I recognized when I heard its [the puppy's] voice.'"

By the time of Socrates (470–399 B.C.E.), the concept of soul had come to include most of the inner life of humanity—the soul was subject to appetites and desires, was the source of emotions and moral values, and was not only the seat of feeling but also of thought. This was a major development, and the soul as one's inner life is a concept that has persisted through to the modern era.

Like the Egyptians and Jews, the Greeks had more than one word for the soul, and possibly believed that each human had more than one soul. They had the notion of *thymos*, the soul as the force that animated the body, as well as the *psyche*, the Greek word most often translated as soul, and the *pneuma*, translated as "spirit." The words *psyche* and *pneuma* were also used by the Gnostics and Christians to differentiate between the two concepts.

The writings of Plato (c. 427–c. 347 B.C.E.), inspired by his mentor, Socrates, form one of the most influential bodies of thought on the soul. Plato neatly summed up the basic view of the soul: "What is it that, when present in a body, makes it living?—a soul."[5] Plato's views on the soul (and those of his teacher Socrates) are not entirely consistent, and they developed through a lifetime of philosophical investigation. The following famous passage about the soul's loss of its wings was obviously an inspiration for the Gnostic doctrine that the soul is drawn down into the body and the material world but should be looking inward and upward to God.

> The soul in her totality has the care of inanimate being everywhere, and traverses the whole heaven in divers forms appearing—when perfect and fully winged she soars upward, and orders the whole world; whereas the imperfect soul, losing her wings and drooping in her flight at last settles on the solid ground—there, finding a home, she receives an earthly frame which appears to be self-moved, but is really moved by her power; and this composition of soul and body is called a living and mortal creature.[6]

As the English poet Shelley commented, Plato was essentially a poet, and his writings are full of vivid images. One of the most famous appears in his dialogue *Phaedrus*, which contains an allegory of the soul as a charioteer on a chariot driven by two horses, one a white horse, which represents the mind, and one a black horse, which represents the body. For Plato, the soul is able to control the mind and the body, at least to the extent that a driver can control his horses.

Also in *Phaedrus* and in *The Republic*, the soul is said to consist of three levels, the rational soul, which is in the head, the passionate or spirited soul, which is in the breast, and the desirous soul, which is in the abdomen. Here, Plato distinguishes between three kinds of impulses that we experience and, because they are part of our inner lives, may be considered to belong to the soul. The division of head, heart, and stomach (or other lower part of the body) is a common one in many spiritual traditions.

Plato had a strong influence on Gnosticism, and many of the following ideas from Plato's dialogue *Timaeus* are to be found in *The Exegesis on the Soul*. In *Timaeus*, the soul has been appointed by God to be "the ruler and mistress of the body." The soul is female here, and it is halfway between divinity and matter. But the soul can be dragged down by the body, and then it acts as if it is drunk, confused by the impermanent world. But when the soul turns away from the confusing and contradictory demands of the material world, "she reflects; then she passes into the realm of purity, and eternity, and immortality, and unchangeableness, which are her kindred, and with them she ever lives, when she is by herself and is not let or hindered; then she ceases from her erring ways, and being in communion with the unchanging is unchanging. And this state of the soul is called wisdom."[7]

Socrates' attempt to prove the immortality of the soul is all the more moving because this dialogue is set immediately before Socrates accepts his death sentence by drinking hemlock. Even though the soul is immortal, it may also go through several lives, and Plato even gives a list of the ten lives through which the soul must travel, the final life being that of the philosopher. Plato's ideas concerning the soul, at least some of which must come from his teacher Socrates, are extensive and have been extraordinarily influential.

Aristotle's Ideas

Aristotle was not a poet, but a scientist. Plato had a massive influence on subsequent Greek and Roman culture. His thought was the basis for the continuing tradition of philosophy. Aristotle's impact on Christianity and Gnosticism, though considerable, was not felt in full until the medieval period. Aristotle was a major figure in medieval Islam and medieval Christianity, and he was known simply as "the philosopher" in educated medieval Christendom. The brilliant twelfth-century Jewish philosopher Maimonides was also an enthusiastic interpreter and adapter of Aristotle's ideas. Aristotle's status as a pagan, who was not Christian, Jewish, or Muslim, caused some consternation to theologians. The great Italian poet Dante knew Aristotle's works well, and he had to place Aristotle, along with the other great classical pagan thinkers, in a limbo, a green shady place that was not in hell, but not in purgatory or paradise either.

Aristotle defined the soul as "that by which we primarily live and perceive and think." This is the soul as interior life, with a hint of the soul as the basic animating principle. One of the difficulties of Plato's view of the soul was that it contrasted with the body. For Plato, the mind, the rational part of the soul, was a fine, elegant white horse, the body a brutish, short-necked, stubborn black horse. As far as Aristotle was concerned, this dichotomy did not adequately express the relationship between the body and the soul. Something of this dichotomy was present in Gnosticism and in many forms of Christianity, but it would have seemed strange to Jewish thinkers, for whom the body, though it would turn to dust, was created by God, as was the soul. The bodily resurrection has persisted as a theme in all three of the monotheistic religions. Aristotle decided that the soul was form to the body's matter. Because all animals might be considered to move and to perceive, Aristotle thought that all living creatures had souls. But there was a hierarchy to this—the human soul could think, whereas animals only had sensory perception and the ability to nourish themselves, while plants had only the latter. He divided the soul into *zoe, psyche*, and *pneuma*, and these suggest, respectively, the soul as vital force, the soul as inner life, and the soul as an element of divinity. As his career developed, Aristotle became less interested in the large ideas that concerned the soul—issues of immortality and the soul's connection with the Divine—and more with the practical, scientific investigation of the subject. In his *de Anima*, Aristotle was fascinated with the idea of sense perception, because touch, taste, smell, sight, and sound are the ways that the soul perceives the external world via the body.

Allegorizing the Soul
The Jewish vision of the soul that longs for God, and returns itself to God, would meet up with the philosophical Greek ideas. It is somewhere around the meeting point of these two that we find the beginnings of Christianity and Gnosticism. There were many Jews spread throughout the Roman Empire, and a particularly strong Jewish community was located in

Alexandria, the Hellenized Egyptian city famous for its vast library, the greatest of the ancient world. Philo of Alexandria was a first-century Jewish writer who wrote vast allegorical commentaries on the Torah. He was inspired by Platonism, and he attempted to bring out the inner meaning of Hebrew scripture by interpreting stories from the Book of Moses using Platonic categories, including soul, spirit, the virtues, and the sensual mind. Early Christian writings, such as the Epistle to the Hebrews and the Gospel of Thomas, are a product of the same Hellenized Jewish world as Philo's writings, and they include a similar use of imagery and metaphor. Gnostics and many early Christians agreed that Philo had discovered something important, for they developed his allegorical techniques and used them to discover their own truths in ancient writings.

Beyond the Gnostics

The Gnostics may be said to have lost the battle for the soul of Christianity. But they left their mark, directly and indirectly, on Christianity. Various Gnostic groups continued in small numbers for centuries, but we only know of their continuing existence through chance references in obscure writings. But the Gnostics had their real successors in the Manichaeans. The prophet Mani lived in the third century and was the founder of a religion that has been dead since the fourteenth century, but it was so widespread, in countries and peoples that range from China to western Europe, that scholars classify it as a world religion. Mani was a Persian from Babylon with connections to Syria, and it seems that he came from a royal background, unless this is meant allegorically. The Manichaean tradition is eclectic, drawing on Buddhism and Zoroastrianism as well as Gnosticism and Christianity. Jesus has an important place in the religion of Mani, and the Gospel of Thomas was used by Manichaeans.

The Manichaean religion shared many ideas with the Gnostics. For example, sparks of light were trapped on earth in humans, and it was the duty of Manichaeans, who seem to have been a somewhat severe people, to separate these light elements from the dark aspects of creation.

Manichaeans were dualists, more so than the Christian Gnostics, ascribing each phenomenon to either a dark or a light origin, and the term *Manichaean* is used to this day to refer to a dualist philosophy or to anything that smacks of a good/bad dichotomy. *The Hymn of the Pearl* may be a Manichaean writing.

Augustine of Hippo, who is often called the greatest Christian theologian, was a Manichaean layman before he converted to Christianity. Augustine was a voluminous writer (though he actually dictated most of his works), and in several tracts he attacks the views of the Manichaeans. However, Augustine's own views on the soul, which were to shape future Western Christianity, were partly influenced by Manichaean ideas and partly in reaction to those ideas. In Manichaeanism, the soul is good and light, and the body is dark and evil, but the soul has fallen and is influenced by the darkness. As an extension of this, there are two souls, one light and the other dark. Augustine argued against this and asserted, in a very Platonic way, that the soul was the *good* of the body. Augustine was able to be thoroughly orthodox in his Christianity, and yet use his intellectual skills to further the definition of Christian concepts. This was the way of Christianity until the Renaissance—intellectual exploration was possible, even admirable, but it needed to stay within the bounds of orthodox dogma. Within these bounds, some of which he created himself, Augustine could even venture that the soul had seven levels—vitality, sensation, art, virtue, tranquility, initiation, and contemplation. His scheme is both Platonic and Christian, and it does include many of the ideas concerning the soul that we have look at so far. For Augustine, the soul was defined by its relation to God, but it had different levels that were progressively closer to God, and so he could acknowledge other properties of the inner world, such as artistic creation.

The Soul in the East

The concepts that developed in Egypt and Greece, and in Judaism, Christianity, and Gnosticism, may be broadly termed the Western tradition, even though Egypt is in Africa and Judaism developed in Asia. Of course, ancient traditions also developed farther east, in ancient China and India and other Asian countries. These have many similarities and also important differences to those ideas that developed in the West, and Eastern religion has had considerable influence on modern Western thought.

Due to the extreme longevity of Indian civilization and its wealth of spiritual material, only the very briefest survey of the main themes is possible here. The Vedas are pre-Hindu scriptures, the collection of which was completed by around 400 B.C.E., although many of them may have been composed a thousand years earlier. They represent the culmination of the earliest stage of Indian religious thought, and we can already see a developed set of soul concepts in these hymns. These concepts correspond very well to the three categories of soul that we have already discussed. The Sanskrit word *asu*, which means "breath of life," is the force that animates the body. The *jiva*, "living being," is one's personality, the soul as the inner psychological world, bound to the body and to the current incarnation. *Manas*, "mind," is a more elevated concept. Transcendent, immaterial, defined by a quality of awareness—it is the soul as spirit.

The Upanishads, teachings based on the Vedas and composed between 700 B.C.E. and 500 B.C.E., are notable for their exaltation of *ātman*, the true self. *Ātman* is beyond reincarnation, it is "nonbeing, uncreated, non-existent, not based on anything, silent.... A wise person therefore never sorrows, for he knows the soul [*ātman*] to be vast, independent and without origin."[8]

The soul as transcendent spirit is a strong theme in Hinduism, and it is often described in extravagant, poetic language. It is an attractive balance and antidote to the Western emphasis of personal responsibility for our own souls. In the epic *Mahabharata*, the Bhagavad Gita is the teaching given by the Krishna, an avatar of the god Vishnu, to the warrior Arjuna just as the great battle is about to commence. Arjuna has been hesitating to go to war, and Krishna, who has been acting as his charioteer, steps forward and reminds Arjuna that the *ātman* is unchangeable and indestructible. Arjuna is then able to face his responsibilities and to act, knowing that the progress and outcome of the events are insignificant in comparison to the greatness of *ātman*.

Buddhism was founded around the sixth century B.C.E in northern India, and is distinctive in its denial of the existence of a soul. In practice this means that it is the reality of the soul as inner world that is being denied. This is a particularly radical variety of the the same viewpoint that places the soul in a subordinate position in Gnosticism. This central tenet of Buddhism becomes less puzzling when we consider that, in comparison with the spirit, the personal soul is unreal. In moments of illumination, many people realize that the wandering thoughts and reactive feelings that we take to be ourselves, are indeed seen as unreal in the light of higher consciousness. And so, from one point of view, there is no individual self, no personal soul, and our internal worlds have no real existence.

Chinese ideas have had less direct influence in the West than have Indian ideas, though Taoism and Chinese medicine have introduced aspects of Chinese spirituality. In early Chinse thought, the *p'o* is the earthly aspect of the soul, the force that animates the body, and the *hun* is the heavenly aspect of the soul, and both of these exist in everyone. The *p'o* and the *hun* correspond somewhat to *yin*, the receptive, feminine principle in the universe, and *yang*, the active, masculine element. According to the traditional Chinese view, everything in the universe is *chi*, whether it is matter or energy, animate or inanimate, organic or inorganic. The universality of *chi* means that a dichotomy between soul and body is somewhat foreign to Chinese thought, and the individuality of the personal soul is less important in traditional Chinese thinking, which looks at humans not so much as individuals but as aspects of the universe and of society. But even in such a different milieu we can see similarities to the familiar concepts of soul, and Chinese folklore contains legends of disembodied spirits whose individual souls have survived death. In the religious traditions, souls may be of different qualities, so that the soul of an emperor is superior to the soul of a peasant. But a soul can improve itself and can ascend, whether through the ethical practices of Confucianism or through the transformative disciplines of Taoism.

The Soul in Islam

While Europe declined as the western Roman Empire collapsed, and Christian civilization was at its strongest in the East, centered in Byzantium and the Byzantine Empire, the new religion of Islam was thriving.

In the Qur'an, the word *ruh*, which is directly related to the Hebrew *ruach*, as both are Semitic languages, means "spirit," specifically the spirit that comes from God. God blows spirit into Adam's clay to animate him, and into Mary's nostrils so that she would conceive Jesus. God's faithful spirit visits Muhammad's heart. As in many of the other religions and cultures that we have examined, the Qur'an also uses a second term, *nafs*, which refers to the human soul, not to the spirit that comes from God. Although these religions and cultures are related to each other—Islam to Christianity and Judaism, Gnosticism to Judaism and Hellenism, Christianity to Judaism, the Greeks to the Egyptians—it is still striking to see how these concepts repeat: Humans have both individual souls and an element of the divine spirit.

The great Sufi poets, such as Rumi and Hafiz, made extensive use of the metaphor of lover and beloved to express what might in other traditions be termed the soul and spirit.

The Soul in Christendom

Medieval Europe was a strange place. Western Europe had been populated for millennia, and the native peoples and cultures had been Romanized to a great or lesser extent as the countries that are now France, Spain, and Britain were incorporated into the Roman Empire. The European Middle Ages experienced a spring in which a vigorous new, fresh culture grew up, but this spring was followed by a sudden winter, in which culture descended rapidly as war and plague took their toll. For a few centuries, western Europe was as intensely religious as the Islamic world, with which it came into contact, an interaction that was both fruitful and murderous. Great thinkers such as Thomas Aquinas adapted Aristotle, who had long been a favorite of Muslims, to Christian thought, just as Augustine had adapted the thought of Plato. According to Thomas Aquinas (c. 1225–74), the soul had three principles—vegetative, sensitive, and rational, but these were three in one, a trinity. To Aquinas, the soul was intimately connected with the body, and even after death the soul was only separate from the body for a while, until the resurrection raised the body and restored it to the soul.

Aquinas' examination of the soul intellectualized the very concrete approach of medieval Christian civilization. The culture that venerated fragments from the true cross or the body parts of saints also had some very literalistic ideas about the soul. Morality plays depicted Satan, Sin, or Death tempting the soul, and engravings showed the soul as it leaves the body, a skinny creature, human in appearance but about a quarter of the size of the host body that has just breathed its last breath. In other illustrations, sinful souls roast in hell, their little arms held up above the flames, their round mouths and open eyes expressing terror.

Dante's tripartite structure of hell, purgatory, and paradise mirrors body, soul, and spirit, and the effect of this earthly life on the future fate of the soul is illustrated poignantly in his *Commedia*. Beatrice perhaps represents his own soul and the idealistic romantic medieval culture of courtly love. Among the many medieval Christian writers who addressed the soul and its qualities, Meister Eckhart stood out as being closer to the Gnostics. His attitude toward the soul corresponded more to the persistent idea that the soul has a spark of divinity in it, but that the soul needs to direct itself toward this inner life instead of outward toward external life. He also used allegorical interpretations of the Bible, and his approach drew accusations of heresy.

Medieval Jewish Views of the Soul

As Christianity and Islam were growing and becoming the dominant religions in Europe and western Asia, Judaism was also developing. The Jerusalem and Babylonian Talmuds, the collections of rabbinical law, commentary, and legend that were completed around the fifth century C.E., elaborated on the role of the soul. The preexistence of the soul was discussed, not without controversy, and the survival and fate of the soul after death was reconciled with the bodily resurrection.

Jewish thinkers in medieval Islamic societies combined Platonic or Aristotelian doctrine with biblical and Talmudic views. Yitshaq Yisrael (c. 850–950 C.E.) divided the soul into rational, animal, and vegetative aspects. Sa'adyah ben Yosef, or Sa'adyah Gaon (c. 882–942 C.E.) reconciled some of the Talmudic views with Islamic philosophy. In the twelfth century, the great Moses Maimonides (1135/8 C.E.–1204 C.E.) adapted an Aristotelian approach. His was a complex analysis of the different components of the soul, a multi-level soul somewhat similar to Augustine's concept, with nutritive, sensitive, imaginative, appetitive, and rational functions. Maimonides distinguished between two different aspects of the rational part of the soul. One aspect of the rational soul involved itself with earthly matters, and the other, the active intellect, concerned itself with divine things and had a direct connection to God. If the active intellect is directed toward contemplation of God and the universe, it becomes the actualized intellect. When the body dies, the actualized intellect becomes immortal, but lower forms of soul perish.

Similar ideas developed within the Jewish mystical system of Kabbalah, where the *nefesh* enters the body at birth and animates it. The *ruach*, the spirit, appears when the desires of the body are overcome. The highest form of soul, the *neshamah*, is formed through the study and application of Torah. These three levels of soul were later connected to the *sefirot* of the tree of life. In these medieval Jewish ideas we see once again varieties of the three typical concepts of the soul, and the understanding that the human soul has different functions within it, and can reach up toward God or remain enmeshed with the concerns of the outer world. Once more we are reminded of the intermediate role of the soul in Gnosticism, midway between the body and the spirit.

The Revival of Learning?

The Renaissance, the revival of learning and the new birth, swept away the medieval world, which, whatever its shortcomings, had a cohesion and consistency to it. The Reformation led to a fragmenting of Christian culture, and the modern secular Western outlook began to develop.

Descartes (1596–1650) certainly did not intend to eliminate the soul from our worldview—quite the opposite, in fact, as he asserted, "This 'I'— that is, the soul, by which I am what I am, is entirely distinct from the body, and would not fail to be what it is even if the body did not exist."[9]

His view was dualistic—the soul and the body were quite separate— but the soul could influence the body through the pineal gland, the only point of contact between the soul and the body. This has been seen as the first step toward the banishment of the soul as an independent entity from modern thought. If the soul and the body are entirely separate, then in a time when scientific discovery, based on the systematic obser- vation of physical phenomena, allows the body to be studied, the soul can be discarded. Descartes' claim that the soul meets the body in the pineal gland was a forerunner of the investigation of the brain, of the understanding that the brain is the organ of thought, and of the study of the mind rather than the soul. In the subsequent history of Western scientific thought, the soul has been ousted by the mind. Philosophers such as Leibnitz, Hobbes, Locke, Berkeley, and Hume continued to spec- ulate on the nature of the soul as mind, and philosophy itself became more secular as science became more dominant. As the concept of mind began to seem inadequate as a description of human inner life, the ques- tion of consciousness took center stage. To the British philosopher George Berkeley (1685–1753), "I my self am not my ideas, but something else, a thinking active principle that perceives, knows, wills and operates about ideas."[10]

As science gathered momentum and the influence of religion declined, the very concept of the soul came into question. Thinking people began to place more faith in the results of physical, empirical science than in the insights and dogma of spirituality and religion. As writer Rosalie Osmond has commented, "We desparately *want* there to be something outside and beyond the physical. Yet, paradoxically, we have to use essentially physical means to attempt to discover this. The result is that the body has grown and the soul has shrunk—some would say to non-existence."[11] Reductionism, whereby all consciousness and mental processes may be ascribed to the brain and other biological causes, has no need of a soul.

The Hidden Soul

The concept of the soul continued to influence heterodox Western thought. The rediscovery of the Hermetic literature, pagan writings contemporary and similar to Gnosticism, had a huge influence on the Renaissance. Movements like Rosicrucianism reintroduced the body-soul-spirit doctrine, which is familiar from Gnosticism. Theosophy brought in ideas such as reincarnation and the different "bodies of man" from Indian and Tibetan religions. The idea of interlocking bodies of increasing fineness, a causal body, a mental body, and an astral body in addition to the physical body, was a new concept in the West. This was another approach to the idea of there being more than one level of soul. In theosophy, the internal life was considered to consist of progressively finer and higher levels, which were characterized as bodies.

The word *psychology* comes from the Greek *psyche* and means "study of the soul." Its use in English goes back to 1693, in a medical dictionary in which the study of the soul is paired with anatomy, the study of the body. *Psyche* itself has a technical meaning in some branches of modern psychology, and in Jungian depth psychology it refers to the inner world in general. In Jungian psychology, the psyche is divided into different qualities or functions. Jung's investigations into the psyche placed his work somewhere between scientific thought and esoteric tradition. Jung was very interested in Gnosticism, and Codex I of the Nag Hammadi library was named the Jung Codex, because the Jung Foundation purchased it from an antiquities dealer.

Of the many esoteric or spiritual influences that have come to light in the West in the twentieth century, the Fourth Way teachings of the Greek Armenian G. I. Gurdjieff and Russian P. D. Ouspensky and their followers contain a number of interesting takes on the soul. Their terminology is not consistent—for instance, Ouspensky often used the word *soul* in reference to the basic vital force, which is a usage that we have seen in various cultures. One of Gurdjieff's most startling teachings was that ordinarily people do not have a soul, though he would sometimes add that we have the seed of a soul that can grow if it is nurtured. This soul must be what we have been calling the spirit, or perhaps the soul as interior world as it strives to connect with spirit. In another place, Gurdjieff referred to the outer world of man, the inner world, and the innermost world, and this corresponds to body, soul, and spirit.

The above examples highlight the renewed interest in sources outside of major religions or scientific thought. Although most of the new religious movements claim some ancient authority for their teachings, ancient teachings themselves have also resurfaced. The discovery at Nag Hammadi in Egypt in 1945 of twelve codices, which comprise a Gnostic library, has given us firsthand evidence of the Gnostic view of the soul.

Among the texts in the Nag Hammadi codices was *The Exegesis on the Soul*. *The Exegesis on the Soul* and *The Hymn of the Pearl*, also Gnostic but not part of the Nag Hammadi library, give important insights into the undeveloped state of the soul and the possibilities that exist for cleansing the soul and directing it once again up toward the divine realm. The Nag Hammadi find and the rediscovery of Gnosticism are having a huge impact on our appreciation of our Western spiritual heritage.

Weighing the Soul

Twentieth- and twenty-first-century attempts to prove the existence of the soul, or to measure it or somehow quantify its existence, have ranged from the rigorous to the absurd. In the early twentieth century, Dr. Duncan McDougall of Massachusetts weighed dying patients and claimed that there was a definite weight loss immediately after death. He became convinced that this was the weight of the departing soul. When he weighed dying dogs he could find no weight loss after the moment of death, and he concluded that dogs had no souls. Though these weights differed, twenty-one grams became the standard weight of the soul, and this inspired a 2003 movie entitled *21 Grams*. One cannot but compare the profound and poetic vision of the ancient Egyptian judgment scene, where the heart is weighed against a feather, to the banal concept of weighing corpses to measure the amount of soul that has escaped the body.

This absurd example is hardly typical of scientific investigation, but scientists are surely barking up the wrong tree if they expect to investigate the soul empirically. The soul is internal, and it should be examined accordingly. Ancient sacred literature such as *The Hymn of the Pearl* and *The Exegesis on the Soul* can tell us more about the soul than any amount of sophisticated scientific analysis can. As in the command of the Delphic Oracle, the first step is to know thyself, to examine our own souls, and the second is to know God, the spirit to which our souls should be connected. The individual soul can reach up to the divine spirit, the two can be made into one, the bride can unite with the bridegroom, and the prince can return to the king of kings.

A Note on the Translation ☐

The Exegesis on the Soul survives in a single Coptic version in Nag Hammadi Codex II. I have used the critical text in Bentley Layton's *Nag Hammadi Codex II, 2–7, vol 1*.

The Hymn of the Pearl survives in Syriac and Greek versions. The translation in the current book is from the Greek, as the Greek version is slightly more Gnostic. The Greek text is taken from Johan Ferreira's edition in *The Hymn of the Pearl: The Syriac and Greek Texts with Introduction, Translations, and Notes*.

I am particularly grateful for Ferreira's translation of *The Hymn of the Pearl* and for William C. Robinson's translation of *The Exegesis on the Soul*. Both of these particularly helped me work through the original texts. For *The Hymn of the Pearl*, I have also consulted the translations of G. R. S. Mead, Marvin Meyer/Willis Barnstone, and others, and for *The Exegesis on the Soul*, I have also consulted the Marvin Meyer/Willis Barnstone version.

In this book, the accurate and unprejudiced term *Hebrew Bible* is used instead of the Christian term *Old Testament*. Because no accurate alternative exists for the term *New Testament*, I refer to the collection by its traditional Christian name.

The Exegesis on
the Soul

☐ Introduction to *The Exegesis on the Soul*

The Exegesis on the Soul is one of the many fascinating pieces of writing that were found at Nag Hammadi. The word *exegesis* is particularly used as a technical term in biblical studies, and it refers to the interpretation of a text, the process of bringing out its meaning. Surprisingly, this unpromising name is actually the title given at the end of the original text. *The Expository Treatise on the Soul* has been suggested as an alternative title, but it is hardly more exciting.

The Exegesis on the Soul is contained in what is now known as Codex II of the Nag Hammadi library. Of the twelve volumes that were found in Egypt in 1945, Codex II is the most important, and it would be no exaggeration to say that had the find consisted of Codex II alone, the discovery would have been just as significant. Codex II opens with *The Apocryphon of John*, perhaps the central text of classic Gnosticism. That is followed by the Gospel of Thomas, which is now the most widely read non-canonical gospel and the most highly considered of the Nag Hammadi texts, and the Gospel of Philip (see my book *The Gospel of Philip: Annotated & Explained* [SkyLight Paths Publishing]), which has been celebrated in Dan Brown's bestseller *The Da Vinci Code*. The remaining texts in Codex II are *The Hypostasis of the Archons* and *On the Origin of the World*, two important Gnostic texts, and *The Book of Thomas the Contender*, a dialogue between Judas Thomas and the Savior, allegedly recorded by one Mathaias.

The Exegesis on the Soul is a work of Christian Gnosticism, and it makes frequent reference to the Hebrew Bible and the Christian New Testament. It does not use the revolutionary inversionary techniques of interpretation typical of classic or Sethian Gnosticism, by means of which the serpent in the Garden of Eden becomes a dispenser of wisdom and the God of the Hebrew Bible becomes the ignorant creator of this fallen world. The approach of *The Exegesis* is closer to the branch of Gnosticism founded by the second-century Alexandrian Gnostic Valentinus.

Valentinian Gnosticism made extensive use of metaphor and allegorical interpretation, and Valentinians saw themselves very much as Christians but as "pneumatic," or "spiritual" Christians, Christians who were connected to the higher spirit and who possessed the inner meaning of scripture—as opposed to merely "psychic" Christians, whose souls were still bound to the world and their own inner lives.

The production of the Nag Hammadi codices can be placed in the mid-fourth century by reference to dates on the packing material used to stiffen the covers. Because writing materials were expensive, scribes often reused papyri, and a few of the papyrus scraps that were recycled for use in these covers were official documents with dates on them. But these allow us to date only the codices, not the texts themselves. This point is often misunderstood by the public and misused by conservative Christian scholars who wish to date Gnostic texts as late as possible. Just because a particular copy of a manuscript was made in the fourth century does not mean that the text itself was composed at that time. In my personal library I have editions of Shakespeare's complete works that were printed in 1896 and 1987 respectively, but neither of these establish the date when Shakespeare wrote his plays.

The early third century c.e. has been suggested as a possible date for the composition of *The Exegesis*. The biblical excerpts are mostly from the prophets—Isaiah, Jeremiah, Hosea—whereas it is the Book of Genesis that is most subject to Gnostic interpretation. The way in which the scriptural quotations are employed suggests the use of a type of anthology known as a florilegium, which was already in use in Alexandria at the beginning of the third century c.e. The mix of Jewish and Greek material in *The Exegesis* is an unusual feature of the text, suggesting a location where both the Bible and Homer were known. The city of Alexandria in Egypt, which was the literary and intellectual capital of the Greek-speaking world, which had a large Jewish population, and which was also the home of the intellectualizing church fathers Clement and Origen, is a likely candidate.

The story that forms the major part of *The Exegesis* follows the soul from her fall from her original virginal androgynous state, during which time she lived with her father. It is her imprisonment in a body (in this case, a female body) that accompanies the fall. She is subjected to sexual degradation, seemingly because of her own negligence. At her lowest ebb, she repents and is forgiven by her father, who sends the bridegroom, who is her older brother (a figure somewhat similar to the older brother in *The Hymn of the Pearl*), and the soul and the spirit or bridegroom unite in the bridal chamber. Interspersed with the story are further meditations on the soul's predicament in this world, as well as interpretations of passages from the Hebrew Bible and Homer. *The Exegesis* is not only telling us the story of the soul's fall and return, it is also showing us how to interpret scripture esoterically, so that we can extract the inner meaning of sacred writings. This method of interpretation is known as allegorization. According to the author of *The Exegesis*, these passages refer not to religious observance or to the state of the Jewish people, but to the condition of the soul and the relationship between the soul and God.

The soul is depicted as a woman in many traditions, but the sympathy for the feminine viewpoint expressed in *The Exegesis* has led scholars to speculate that the author may have been female. Whether the author was female or male, and regardless of the reader's own gender, we are expected to imagine ourselves in the position of the soul, who gives herself away to thieves and adulterers, and yet by repentance and the grace of the father can enter the bridal chamber and unite with the bridegroom in a final marriage of soul and spirit.

1   *The Exegesis* was written in the late second or early third century, yet, even to the author, the concept of the soul as a feminine figure is ancient. The sources of ancient wisdom that the author has in mind are the Hebrew Bible (particularly the prophets) and the epics of Homer.

2   The unnamed female figure in *The Exegesis* is passive, and in the course of her life she is bound to the ancient role of womanhood— she is safe until she leaves her father; her promiscuity is an aspect of her fall, particularly because the men with whom she has sex are unworthy of her. She is restored by marrying the bridegroom and returning to her father. Thus, her fall and return is entirely dependent on the masculine figures with whom she consorts. This ancient Mediterranean view of womanhood differs considerably from modern Western standards, but it must be understood by the modern reader so that the metaphor can work.

3   At the beginning of *The Exegesis*, the soul is genderless and virginal. By the end, she has united with the bridegroom in the bridal chamber. The soul's initial virginity corresponds to the childhood of the prince in *The Hymn of the Pearl*. Her virginity is lost to the thieves with whom she copulates, but it is restored when she repents, and her subsequent union with the bridegroom does not seem to affect her virginal state. The soul's journey, harrowing though it is, results in maturity and development.

Androgyny, the state of being male and female in one, is a common image in Gnosticism and related writings. The image of androgny has been used and interpreted in a variety of ways over the centuries. According to the modern Jungian view, it refers to the need to balance the male and female aspects of our psychology. In ascetic traditions, such as monastic Christianity, androgyny is equivalent to the state of celibacy, for when one is celibate, one is neither male nor female. But in the Gnostic interpretation, androgyny is the state of the female soul united with the masculine spirit.

☐ The Exegesis on the Soul

In ancient times,[1] the wise referred to the soul as feminine. Even her nature is female.[2] She even has a womb.

While she lived alone with the father, she was a virgin and her form was androgynous.[3]

(continued on page 9)

4 Note that the soul "fell down" into a body. *The Exegesis* does not explain why the soul had to fall. In *The Hymn of the Pearl*, the fall is a result of the prince being unable to keep to his mission and accepting the food and clothing of the Egyptians. In Gnosticism, as in Platonism, the body is generally seen as a prison for the soul. Other traditions, such as Judaism, much of Christianity, and the philosophical tradition of Aristotle and his followers, regarded the relationship between the soul and the body as less antagonistic.

5 The thieves could remind us of the parable of the Good Samaritan, in which a traveling Samaritan is robbed and left for dead. There have been many allegorical interpretations of the Good Samaritan. The early church fathers, Irenaeus (second century), Origen (third century), and Ambrose and Augustine (both fourth century), have each contributed extensive interpretations. In Origen's interpretation, the Samaritan is Jesus; in Augustine's, the wounded traveler is the fallen soul.

6 The Gospel of Philip 43 gives us a capitulation of this theme. "So also the lecherous men, when they see a beautiful woman sitting alone, they persuade her and compel her, wishing to defile her. But if they see the man and his wife sitting beside one another, the female cannot come into the man, nor can the male come into the woman."

✦ The thieves use two methods to abuse the soul—violence and seduction. Regardless of the method, the soul ends up defiled. The two methods that the thieves use may represent both the pleasant and unpleasant things that pull us away from the life of the spirit. On a practical level, the violence of the thieves may be our minor irritations and negative emotions, whereas the seduction may represent our trivial fascinations.

But when she fell downward into a body[4] and came into this life, then she found herself in the hands of thieves.[5] And these perverted men passed her from one to the other and abused her. Some of them took her violently, while others seduced her with presents. They defiled her, and she lost her virginity.[6]

(continued on page 11)

7 In a realistic touch, the soul's post-coital depression drives her to further promiscuity.

8 What are the thieves and adulterers meant to represent here? In other Gnostic myths and stories, it is the archons who prevent the soul from ascending. The Greek word *archon* may be translated as "ruler," though in many translations of Gnostic material it is rendered untranslated, written simply as "archon." The archons are the thoughts and desires which distract the soul from her ascent to the spirit.

9 *The Exegesis on the Soul* is allegorical, and the main elements of the story are intended to explain, by the use of metaphor, how the soul becomes ensnared by the body and the outside world, and yet can turn away from these lower influences and experience the world of the spirit. In modern society, few of us are able to withdraw completely from the world, and few of us wish to deny our bodies in an ascetic way. Most of our basic needs, such as the need for food, drink, clothing, sex, and accommodation, are generated by our bodies, and we may often feel submerged by the demands of life, earning money, and paying bills. "Getting and spending we lay waste our powers," as Wordsworth puts it. Yet many spiritual disciplines can make it possible to fulfill the requirements of life, to be "in the world, yet not of it" as the Sufis put it.

And she whored herself in her body and gave herself to anyone, treating each man she was about to embrace as her husband. When she had given herself to these perverted, unfaithful, and adulterous men, and they had taken her, then she sighed within and repented. Yet even when she turned her face away from those adulterous men, she rushed to others,[7] who made her live with them and made her service them on their beds, as if they were her lords.[8] She no longer tried to leave them because she was so ashamed, and for a long time they deceived her, pretending to be true and faithful husbands. But afterward they each abandoned her and departed.[9]

(continued on page 13)

10 The soul is now designated as being a widow—a woman whose husband is dead. Perhaps she is similar to the Samarian woman at the well in the Gospel of John. Jesus said to her, "Go, call your husband, and come here." The woman answered him, "I have no husband." Jesus said to her, "You are right in saying, 'I have no husband'; for you have had five husbands, and he whom you now have is not your husband; this you said truly" (John 4:16–18 RSV). The Gospel of John may have strong affinities with Gnosticism, and the woman at the well is often equated with the soul.

11 The sexual morality presented in this story is quite a conventional one, and most Christians would approve of it. The early church fathers tended to accuse Gnostics of being either ascetic sex-haters or orgiastic libertines, yet the view of sex given here is one of moderation. Meaningless promiscuity is abhorred, but the faithful union of the bride and groom in the bridal chamber is the culmination of the soul's existence.

12 The soul's promiscuity has left her with nothing. Her children are blind, mute, sick (all sicknesses that are cured by Jesus in the healing miracles), and stupid. In the ancient world, it was commonly thought that the manner of lovemaking or the things that one saw while making love affected the resulting baby. These children are never mentioned again, but once the soul has met the bridegroom, we are told that she can bear good children.

Allegorically, what could it mean that the soul's children are blind, mute, and stupid? If we take the soul as the inner life, then its children are thoughts, emotions, and perceptions. The thoughts and emotions generated by the random distractions of life are blind, dumb, and dense, but the thoughts and feelings that are a result of the connection with the spirit are healthy and good and have a future. The Gospel of Philip 95 sums this up: "The children born of a woman will resemble the man whom she loves. If it is her husband whom she loves, then her husband will love her; if it is an adulterer, then they will resemble the adulterer."

Then she became a poor, helpless, barren widow.[10] There was not even any food left for her from the time of her abuse. She received nothing from them except the defilement they gave her while they had sex with her.[11] She had children by the adulterers, and they are mute, blind, and weak.

They are stupid.[12]

(continued on page 15)

13 This father is an ancient Near Eastern father, who keeps his women in their quarters.

The soul left her father's house of her own accord, and admits her mistake. Her "father from above" shows mercy to her and does not chastise her for leaving her home.

14 June Singer, the late Gnostic Jungian, contrasted the viewpoints of *The Exegesis on the Soul* and *The Hymn of the Pearl*: "The soul, being reflective, is painfully aware of her separation and alienation, while at the beginning of *The Hymn of the Pearl*, the prince, as ego, is blissfully unaware of the purpose of his journey."

15 The story of the soul's journey has reached a critical point. Having fallen to her lowest level, she is now repenting and begins her return to the father. This is heartfelt language, and the author of *The Exegesis* is not merely writing a clever allegory, but must have also experienced emotions corresponding to the soul's degradation and repentance. This sympathy with the plight of the feminine soul may indicate that the author is female.

But when her father from above visited her and looked down on her and saw her sighing, and her suffering and shame, and he saw her repent of her prostitution, and when she began to call on his name, for him to give her help, she cried out with all her heart, saying, "My father, save me, my father, for I will be honest with you, I left my home and escaped from the women's quarters.[13] Bring me back to you again." When he saw her in such a state,[14] then he considered her worthy of his mercy, for she had endured many trials since she had left her home.[15]

16 The next portion of *The Exegesis on the Soul* interprets scripture from this allegorical point of view. The quotations from the Hebrew Bible have been translated into Coptic, most likely from the Greek Septuagint, which is itself a translation from Hebrew. There is also a certain amount of interpretation going on, so these quotations are quite different from the passages that we now find in the Bible. It is more accurately a free paraphrase rather than a quotation. In this translation, the renderings of biblical passages are based on the Revised Standard Version (RSV), but vary from the RSV roughly to the extent that the Coptic version in *The Exegesis* varies.

17 The passage from Jeremiah mirrors the progress of the soul. Jeremiah contrasts the true husband with the many shepherds. The separation of soul and spirit is caused by the husband (the spirit) divorcing the wife (the soul). Once the soul had fallen she "played the harlot to many shepherds" and made herself unclean. In *The Exegesis* the divorce is only temporary, and the soul ultimately returns to the bridegroom.

18 Jeremiah 3:1–4. Some commentators have suggested that the quotations are taken from an ancient anthology. Anthologies were popular in the ancient world for much the same reasons as they are today—books are expensive and take time to read, so there are advantages in reading collected excerpts instead. If the quotations are indeed extracts from a collection (and they may also just be quoted by memory), then *The Exegesis* may have been written in Alexandria in the late second or early third century, since these anthologies were known to have been popular around that time.

Now, the Holy Spirit prophesies about the soul's prostitution in many places. For it is said in the prophet Jeremiah,[16]

> If the husband divorces his wife and she goes from him and takes another man, can she subsequently return to him? Has not that woman made herself unclean? "And you played the harlot to many shepherds and you returned to me!" said the Lord. "Lift up your eyes and see where you prostituted yourself. Were you not sitting in the streets making the land unclean with your harlotry and vices? And you took many shepherds as a stumbling block for yourself.[17] You were shameless with everyone. You did not call on me as family or as father or creator of your virginity."[18]

19 The passage from Hosea (2:2–7) is much closer to the biblical version. It is a powerful, if severe, piece of writing.

Hosea was married to an unfaithful wife, Gomer, and Hosea uses this as an allegory of the relationship between Israel and God and, by extension, between the individual soul and God. Each of the children conceived by Gomer was given a name with unpleasant associations. Their son, Jezreel, was named after a valley associated with King Ahab, where Ahab's seventy sons were killed. Their daughters were Loruhamah, Hebrew for "not pitied" and Loammi, "not of my people."

The "children of harlotry" are equivalent to the offspring of the soul mentioned previously in *The Exegesis*.

20 All of the passages quoted in *The Exegesis* are intended to be interpreted allegorically. The author is showing how the Hebrew Bible can be understood as a vast collection of allegorical passages that refer to the soul's fall and return. Many of these biblical passages were intended by their authors to be interpreted allegorically, or at least meant to be interpreted in terms of the unfaithfulness of Israel. It may be an interesting exercise for the reader to pick out other passages from the Hebrew Bible or the New Testament, and to see whether they can be interpreted as describing the plight of the soul.

✦ "[In *The Exegesis*] the soul as bride is cleansed and renewed. She is restored to her virginity, and all that she has suffered is like a horrific dream that vanishes in the light of dawn."

—June Singer, *A Gnostic Book of Hours*, p. 105.

It is written also in the prophet Hosea,[19]

> Come, plead with your mother, for she is not my
> wife nor am I her husband to her. I shall remove her
> harlotry from my presence, and her adultery from
> between her breasts. I shall strip her naked as the day
> she was born, and I shall make her barren like a
> waterless land, and I shall make her childless yet she
> shall long for children. I shall show her children no
> pity, for they are children of harlotry, since their
> mother sold herself and put her children to shame.
> For she said, "I shall sell myself to my lovers. It was
> they who gave me my bread and water and garments
> and my clothes and wine and oil and everything I
> needed." Therefore I shall shut them up so that she
> shall not be able to seek her adulterers. And when
> she seeks them and does not find them, she will say,
> "I shall return to my previous husband, for in those
> days I was better off than I am now."[20]

21 Ezekiel 16:23–26. Ezekiel's prophecies in particular have been interpreted in terms of spiritual allegory. Perhaps these visions and admonitions had a deeper level, beyond the level of national allegory, and might be considered allegories of the soul. The author of *The Exegesis* certainly thought so. Jewish *merkabah* mysticism is based on the vision of the chariot in Ezekiel, and the twelfth-century Jewish philosopher Maimonides wrote extensive commentary on various aspects of Ezekiel's visions.

22 *The Exegesis* gives us a direct interpretation of "sons of Egypt ... men great of flesh" as being the bodily things and external concerns that distract the soul. Egypt here represents the fallen world, just as it does in *The Hymn of the Pearl*.

23 In *The Hymn of the Pearl,* the hero is also given food, from the Egyptians, which results in his falling asleep and forgetting his mission. "Bread, wine, oil, and clothing" are all common images in the Bible, particularly in the Gospels. These are all essentials of Mediterranean life, and are generally positive symbols. The soul's acceptance of these from the thieves and adulterers is linked intimately with her fall and degradation.

✦ The words of the "the apostles of the Savior" are not a direct quotation, but may refer to a number of passages in the writings of Paul or in the Acts of the Apostles, such as Acts 15:20, 15:29, 21:25; 1 Thessalonians 4:3; 1 Corinthians 6:18; and 2 Corinthians 7:1. Each of these passages commends us to avoid sexual immorality.

Once more he said in Ezekiel,[21]

> "After much depravity," said the Lord, "it happened that you built a brothel and you made yourself a beautiful place in the streets. And you built yourself brothels on every lane, you squandered your beauty, and you opened your legs in every alleyway, and you multiplied your acts of harlotry. You whored yourself to the sons of Egypt, those who are your neighbors, men great of flesh."[22]

But what does "the sons of Egypt, men great of flesh" mean, other than the realm of the flesh and the material world and earthly things, by which the soul has become unclean, accepting bread from them, and wine, oil, clothing, and the other external garbage surrounding the body—those things she thinks are essential.[23]

But as to this prostitution, the apostles of the Savior commanded, "Protect yourselves against it, purify yourselves from it," speaking not just of the prostitution of the body but particularly that of the soul. Because of this the apostles wrote to the churches of God, that this harlotry should not occur with us.

24 Prostitution, of course, involves providing sexual favors in exchange for money or other material compensation. That is, selling what is potentially among our most precious and intimate experiences to anyone who comes along. In the ancient world, there were various forms of sacred prostitution, in addition to the common form of prostitution for money. Both forms of prostitution existed in ancient Israel, and Hosea, Ezekiel, and Jeremiah are noted for their virulent condemnation of prostitution.

25 Here the author is quoting from Paul's letter 1 Corinthians 5:9–10.

26 Here the author is quoting from Ephesians 6:12, a letter that is attributed to Paul, though many scholars have disputed the authorship.

27 We have returned to the story of the soul. To modern sensibilities, the sections on biblical interpretation may seem to wander away from the central myth of *The Exegesis*. But these passages are an essential part of the author's purpose. The author wants the reader to understand scripture esoterically, as relating to the soul, and has provided these examples as a guide to interpretation. We cannot claim historically that the original biblical writers had the soul in mind when they wrote these passages, but the author of *The Exegesis* was certainly convinced that this was the case.

28 Since the soul is female, she has a womb. Initially, the soul's womb is on the outside, because the soul's attention is directed toward external things, not inward toward the spirit. Clearly, a womb that is open and on the outside cannot conceive, and so the soul's external womb cannot lead to a new birth.

But the greatest fight has to do with the prostitution of the soul. From this the prostitution of the body occurs.[24] So Paul, writing to the Corinthians, said, "I wrote you in my letter, 'Do not associate with prostitutes,' not at all intending the prostitutes of this world or the greedy or the thieves or the idolaters, since then you would need to go out from the world"[25]—here he is speaking spiritually—"For we struggle not against flesh and blood," as he said, "but against the world rulers of this darkness and the spirits of evil."[26]

As long as the soul keeps wandering around copulating with anyone she meets and making herself unclean, she receives her appropriate punishment.[27] But when she perceives the difficulties she has, and weeps before the father and repents, then the father will have mercy on her and he will turn her womb away from the outer world and turn it inward so that the soul will regain her correct form. It is not like this with a woman. The body's womb is inside the body like the other organs, but the soul's womb is on the outside like the male genitals, which are external.[28]

(continued on page 25)

29 Baptism is compared to the washing of clothes. We have already seen that, in the imagery of Gnosticism, and sometimes also Judaism and early Christianity, clothes represent our psychological states. The ritual of baptism may be interpreted as a kind of initiation, or as a washing away of sins, but in each example it represents a new beginning, and here it is the beginning of the soul's ascent.

30 Gospel of John 16:21. "When a woman is in travail she has sorrow, because her hour has come; but when she is delivered of the child, she no longer remembers the anguish, for joy that a child is born into the world." This is spoken by Jesus in the context of his departure and return (16:16), "A little while, and you will see me no more; again a little while, and you will see me." The experience of the disciples between the time of Jesus' death and the resurrection is somewhat similar to the plight of the soul between her leaving the father and her return to the bridegroom.

31 The cleansing of the soul, her baptism, and the turning within of the womb are merely preparation. In a strange variation on the image of pregnancy, the soul is in labor, in the pangs of childbirth, yet she cannot deliver her child because she has not yet conceived.

32 The baptism of the soul is followed by the soul's entry into the bridal chamber. Both baptism and the rite of the bridal chamber (which was not necessarily a sexual practice) were important sacraments in Gnosticism, in addition to their metaphorical meanings. The Gospel of Philip 60 mentions five sacraments; Philip section 60 tells us that "The Lord did everything in a mystery: a baptism and a chrism and a eucharist and a redemption and a holy bridal chamber." The chrism (anointing with oil) and eucharist are not mentioned specifically in *The Exegesis*, although the soul consumes the wine, bread, and oil of the thieves and adulterers. Redemption is also important in *The Exegesis*, although it is not explicitly a sacrament.

So when the soul's womb, by the will of the father, turns itself inward, it is baptized and is immediately cleansed of the outer pollution which was pressed on it, just as dirty clothing is put into the water and turned about until the dirt is removed and it becomes clean.[29] And so the purpose of the cleansing of the soul is to regain the newness of her earlier nature and to turn back again. That is her baptism.

Then she will begin to cry like a woman in labor, who writhes and cries out in the pain of birth.[30] But because she is female, she is unable to beget a child by herself. So the father sent her husband from heaven.[31] He is her brother, he is the firstborn. Then the bridegroom came down to the bride. She gave up her former prostitution and cleansed herself of the uncleanness of the adulterers, and she was renewed so as to be a bride. She cleansed herself in the bridal chamber,[32] she filled it with fragrance, and she sat down, waiting for the true bridegroom. She has stopped running around the marketplace, copulating with anyone, but she continues to wait for him.

(continued on page 27)

33 The soul must wait patiently for the bridegroom. Turning aside from her adulteries—external concerns—has simply prepared her for this intermediate situation, where she experiences the pangs of birth and yet is waiting patiently for the bridegroom. These unusual, acausal aspects of *The Exegesis*, in which the logical development of the story is interrupted, remind us that the story is here to explain the workings of the soul. The process of directing our inner psychological world toward the immediate, living experience of the spirit, and away from the labyrinth of the outside world, is not a linear one. The spirit is the brother, husband, and perhaps also the child of the soul. The soul loses her virginity and regains it. She gives birth to damaged children who are never referred to again. She has birth pangs even before she has conceived.

✦ Physical lovemaking is contrasted with spiritual marriage. The climax of sex is followed by an uncoupling and separation, and while satisfied lovers need not turn their faces away from each other, as suggested in *The Exegesis*, post-coital lovers are not as intensely together as they were during the lovemaking. Not so with the spiritual marriage, where the soul and the spirit are united forever.

The Gospel of Philip similarly contrasts fleshly and spiritual marriage: "For marriage in the world is a mystery for those who have married. If the defiled marriage is hidden, how much more is the undefiled marriage a true mystery. It is not fleshly but holy; it does not belong to desire but to the will. It does not belong to the darkness and the night, but to the day and the light."

"When will he come?" she said, and she was afraid of him, because she did not recall his appearance since the time when she fell from her father's house.[33] But by the will of the father […] And she dreamed of him, as if she were a woman in love with a man.

But then the bridegroom, by the will of the father, came down to her in the bridal chamber, which she had made ready. And he decorated the bridal chamber.

Since that marriage is not like the bodily marriage, those who are to make love with one another will be satisfied with that form of lovemaking. And as if it were a duty, leaving behind them the upset of carnal desire, they turn their faces from each other. But in this marriage, once they unite with each other, they become a single life. This is why the prophet said about the first man and the first woman, "They will become a single flesh." For they were originally joined together when they were with the father, before the woman led astray the man, who is her brother. This marriage has brought them back together again and the soul has been joined to her true love, her real master, as it is written, "For the master of the woman is her husband."

(continued on page 29)

34 When the prince in *The Hymn of the Pearl* first returns home, he cannot remember his former state either. She does not recognize her brother at first. This is also true of us. We begin with a vague feeling that there is a more spiritual reality, and that by loosening our attachments to worldly things we have more chance of experiencing the life of the spirit, yet a good deal of patience and longing for a higher perception of reality is required.

35 The bridegroom is also the soul's older brother. In *The Hymn of the Pearl*, the prince also has a mysterious older brother who seems to be connected with the spirit and who remains in the prince's kingdom. If we take this literally, the soul is in an incestuous relationship, but allegorically this expresses something about the soul's relationship to the spirit. The spirit is the older brother of the soul, but this soul has separated from the spirit, and the soul's reuniting with the spirit is described as a marriage. This same connection can be found in the Hebrew and Christian scriptures. In the Song of Solomon, the beloved is told, "You have ravished my heart, my sister, my bride, you have ravished my heart with a glance of your eyes, with one jewel of your necklace" (Song 4:9 RSV). In 1 Corinthians 9:5, Paul also refers to a sister-wife. Many translations obscure this by rendering it as "a believing wife" (NIV and others), "a Christian wife" (New American Bible), or just "a wife" (RSV). The King James Version translates this literally as "Have we not power to lead about a sister, a wife, as well as other apostles, and as the brethren of the Lord, and Cephas?" Paul's usage may also be metaphorical—and Gnostics would certainly have interpreted it so.

36 Here the author is quoting from Psalm 45:10–11.

Slowly she recognized him,[34] and once again she felt joy, as she wept before him while she remembered the shame of her previous widowhood. And she beautified herself even more so that he would be happy to stay with her.[35]

For the prophet said in the Psalms. "Hear, my daughter, and see and incline your ear and forget your people and your father's house, and the king will desire your beauty, since he is your lord."[36]

(continued on page 31)

`37` Genesis 12:1. In Genesis, this quotation is followed by the wander-
ings of Abraham and his family, which eventually lead them to Egypt.
Abraham claims that Sarah is his sister, not his wife, fearing that the
Egyptians will kill him so that they can take his wife. This leads to the
Lord sending plagues to the pharaoh and his people. Pharaoh rebukes
Abraham, "Why did you say, 'She is my sister,' so that I took her for my
wife? Now then, here is your wife, take her, and be gone" (RSV).
Although this passage is not quoted explicitly, it clearly resonates with
the theme of the soul being both the sister and the wife of the bridegroom, and the story of Abraham and Sarah in Egypt mirrors the
descent of the soul and her whoredom in the material world. Sarah was
"taken into the pharaoh's house" in return for Abraham receiving
"sheep, oxen, he-asses, menservants, maidservants, she-asses, and
camels" (Gen. 12:15–16). This recalls the soul's exchange of sexual
favors for food and clothing.

`◆` "[*The Exegesis*] follows the scheme of redemption of such sinners
as Ruth, Tamar, Rahab and Bathsheba. Centering on women's redemption was also typical of other Jewish literature of the time, including
documents recounting the experience of the soul in the Essene texts
found at Qumran."

—Willis Barnstone and Marvin Meyer, *The Gnostic Bible*, p. 406.

For he demands that she should turn her face away from her people and the crowd of adulterers, in whose midst she once was, to devote herself to her king, the real lord, and to forget the house of the earthly father, with whom things went badly for her, but to remember her father who is in heaven. This is why it was said to Abraham: "Go from your country and your kindred and your father's house."[37]

(continued on page 33)

38 Finally, the bridegroom comes down to meet the bride within the bridal chamber. The bridal chamber is a powerful metaphor in Gnosticism and early Christianity; see, for instance, the parable of the bridegroom in Mark 2:18–22: "Now John's disciples and the Pharisees were fasting; and people came and said to him, 'Why do John's disciples and the disciples of the Pharisees fast, but your disciples do not fast?' And Jesus said to them, 'Can the wedding guests fast while the bridegroom is with them? As long as they have the bridegroom with them, they cannot fast. The days will come, when the bridegroom is taken away from them, and then they will fast in that day.'"

39 Since the bridegroom's seed or semen is life-giving spirit, we can assume that the groom is to be identified with the spirit. With respect to the spirit, our own souls are considered to be the feminine, passive aspect of the partnership, just as God is sometimes said to be the bridegroom of the Jewish people, or the church the bride of Christ.

Various traditions have speculated when and how the soul enters this world. The second- and third-century church father Tertullian held a doctrine that he called "traducianism," which held that the soul entered the body via the father's sperm.

40 The soul is female (in this text, at least) and lacks the male element that is necessary for her conception. Her deformed children, the result of her whorish dalliances, have been forgotten by this point in the narrative, emphasizing that they should be interpreted allegorically.

Thus when the soul had beautified herself, she enjoyed her beloved, and he loved her too.[38] And when she made love with him, she received his seed,[39] the life-giving spirit, so that she can bear good children by him and she can rear them. For this is the great and perfect wonder that is birth. And so the will of the father made the marriage perfect.[40]

(continued on page 35)

41 The statement that the soul moves of her own accord may derive from Plato. "The soul through all her being is immortal, for that which is ever in motion is immortal; but that which moves another and is moved by another, in ceasing to move ceases also to live. Only the self-moving, never leaving self, never ceases to move, and is the fountain and beginning of motion to all that moves besides."

42 The ascent toward the father is not primarily a matter of personal achievement; it is due to the grace of the father. In *The Hymn of the Pearl*, the hero has completely forgotten his mission and it is only the letter from Persia that reminds him of it.

43 Psalm 103:1–5. Some of the above images were taken from Psalm 103, which the author now quotes directly.

44 The author pulls together many strands of symbolism. In making love with the bridegroom, the soul receives her father's divinity, which rejuvenates and regenerates her. She is born again. We are clearly told that this is the same process and result as the resurrection of the dead, and of being ransomed or redeemed. For Christians, the resurrection of the dead is a real event that will happen in the end days, in which our physical bodies will actually be brought back to life in some way. For the Gnostics, the resurrection of the dead happened in this life, since the soul that is separated from the spirit can be considered dead.

45 "Repeated phrases" may be a reference to prayer, but the Gnostics also were criticized by various anti-Gnostic commentators for memorizing lists of passwords to be given to the archons. In some Gnostic cosmologies, these passwords, seals, or secret names were spoken to the archons to allow the soul to ascend through the levels of heaven.

46 Gospel of John 6:44.

WIN A
$100
GIFT
CERTIFICATE!

Fill in this card and
mail it to us—
or fill it in online at

**skylightpaths.com/
feedback.html**

—to be eligible for a
$100 gift certificate for
SkyLight Paths books.

SKYLIGHT PATHS PUBLISHING
SUNSET FARM OFFICES RTE 4
PO BOX 237
WOODSTOCK VT 05091-0237

Fill in this card and return it to us to be eligible for our quarterly drawing for a $100 gift certificate for SkyLight Paths books.

We hope that you will enjoy this book and find it useful in enriching your life.

Book title: _____

Your comments: _____

How you learned of this book: _____

If purchased: Bookseller _____ City _____ State _____

Please send me a free SKYLIGHT PATHS Publishing catalog. I am interested in: (check all that apply)

1. ❑ Spirituality
2. ❑ Mysticism/Kabbalah
3. ❑ Philosophy/Theology

4. ❑ Spiritual Texts
5. ❑ Religious Traditions (Which ones?)
_____
6. ❑ Children's Books

7. ❑ Prayer/Worship
8. ❑ Meditation
9. ❑ Interfaith Resources

Name (PRINT) _____

Street _____

City _____ State _____ Zip _____

E-MAIL (FOR SPECIAL OFFERS ONLY) _____

Please send a SKYLIGHT PATHS Publishing catalog to my friend:

Name (PRINT) _____

Street _____

City _____ State _____ Zip _____

SKYLIGHT PATHS® Publishing Tel: (802) 457-4000 • Fax: (802) 457-4004

Available at better booksellers. Visit us online at www.skylightpaths.com

Now it is right that the soul should regenerate herself and that she should be once more what she formerly was. Then the soul moved of her own volition.[41] She received the father's divine nature for her rejuvenation, so that she should be restored to her original status. This is the resurrection from the dead. This is the ransom from captivity. This is the journey of the ascent to heaven, and the way of ascent to the father.[42] For this reason the prophet said:

> Bless the lord, O my soul, and, all that is within me, bless his holy name! My soul, bless God, who forgives all your iniquity, who heals all your diseases, who redeems your life from the pit, who crowns you with mercy, who satisfies your longing with good, so that your youth is renewed like an eagle's.[43]

Then when she becomes young again, she will ascend, praising the father and her brother who rescued her. This is how, by being born again, the soul will be saved.[44] And this is due not to repeated phrases or to professional skills or to book learning.[45] Rather it is due to the grace of the father, and it is a gift from the father, for it is a heavenly thing. This is why the Savior cries out, "No one can come to me unless the Father who sent me draws him, and brings him to me; and I will raise him up on the last day."[46]

(continued on page 37)

47 The vocabulary here—sighing, repenting, confessing, weeping, and mourning—also sounds very Christian. Christian Gnostics thought of themselves primarily as Christians, but they felt that they were pneumatic, spiritual Christians rather than psychic, conventional Christians. Pneumatic Christians had access to the spirit, but psychic Christians were stuck at the level of the soul, which, in the absence of the spirit, can only be concerned with material things.

48 This beatitude is put together from those found in Matthew 5:4 and Luke 6:21, with a few variations. As such, it might be considered an agraphon, a saying of Jesus that is not found in the New Testament.

49 Compare Luke 14:26. In the context of *The Exegesis*, hating one's own soul has a very specific meaning. This is the spiritless soul, the soul who whores herself in the material world.

50 Compare with Acts 13:24. This is the only reference to Christ in the text. Just as John the Baptist precedes Christ, so does redemption precede salvation, and repentance precede the bridal chamber.

51 This appears to be taken from 1 Clement 8:3, the letter of Clement of Rome to the Corinthians, written around the end of the first century. Clement may in turn be quoting an unidentified passage, which uses the language of the Hebrew prophets. In biblical language, the color red is often identified with lust, and the color black with mourning.

52 This quotation is taken from Isaiah 30:15.

So it is right to pray to the father and to call on him with all our soul —not outwardly with the lips, but with the inner spirit, which came forth sighing from the depths, repenting for the life we lived. Confessing our sins, understanding our self-deceit, and our empty enthusiasm, weeping over the darkness and the wave we were in; mourning for ourselves, so we might be pitied. Hating ourselves for the way that we are now.[47]

Again the Savior said, "Blessed are those who mourn, for they shall be pitied; blessed are those who hunger now, for they will be satisfied."[48]

Again he said, "Anyone who does not hate his soul cannot follow me."[49] For the beginning of salvation is repentance. Therefore, "Before the appearance of Christ, John came, preaching the baptism of repentance."[50]

And repentance happens when there is trouble and sorrow. But the father is good and he loves humanity, and hears the soul that calls upon him and sends the light of salvation. This is why he said by the spirit to the prophet, "Tell the children of my people, 'If your sins reach from earth to heaven, and if they become red like scarlet and blacker than sackcloth, and if you turn to me with all your soul and say to me "Father!," I will listen to you as a holy people.'"[51]

Again elsewhere, "For thus said the lord, the holy one of Israel: 'In returning and sighing, you shall be saved, and you will know where you were when you trusted in emptiness.'"[52]

(continued on page 39)

53 This quotation is taken from Isaiah 30:19–20. We may wonder whether the author has fashioned the details of her narrative around these scriptural quotations, or based the narrative on generally known symbolism, and then looked for confirmation of her point of view in scripture.

54 Sea travel was extensive in the ancient world. Sea routes were much faster than land routes, but sea travel was very dangerous. Both Paul and Augustine suffered shipwrecks. Prayers made at sea were obviously meant very sincerely. Metaphorically, a small boat in the sea mirrors the state of the soul in the world.

55 The material world is seen as "a place of deception."

56 The author now moves to exegesis of extracts from Homer, who is referred to simply as "the poet" (Homer, *The Odyssey* 1.48–59). The works of Homer were the foundation of the Greek education that was given to the educated citizens of the Roman Empire. Homer's importance to the Greek-speaking culture of that time may be considered to lie somewhere between the importance of the King James Bible and Shakespeare in well-educated English-speaking cultures. In the early centuries, and also in later Byzantine literature, Homer was interpreted allegorically. Plutarch and Porphyry and the author of *The Homeric Allegories* were among the allegorical interpreters. Porphyry was a third-century neo-Platonist who was familiar with Gnostic teachings. In his interpretation of *The Odyssey*, Odysseus, the wandering survivor of the Trojan war who was trying to return home, represented the soul. Just as we look to ancient texts such as the Bible or the Nag Hammadi library and find in them profound meaning that we feel is relevant to our contemporary lives, so too the ancients reinterpreted the foundation texts of their own cultures.

Elsewhere again, "Jerusalem wept much, saying, 'Have pity on me.' He will have pity on the sound of your weeping. And when he saw, he listened to you. And though the Lord will give you bread of adversity and the water of affliction, from now on, those who deceive will not come near you again. Your eyes will see those who deceive you."[53]

So it is right to pray to God night and day, spreading out our hands toward him like people sailing in the middle of the sea. They pray to God with all their heart without hypocrisy.[54] For those who pray hypocritically deceive only themselves. Indeed, it is so that he might know who deserves salvation that God examines the inner parts and searches the depths of the heart. For no one who still loves the place of deception is worthy of salvation.[55]

Therefore it is written in the poet, "Odysseus sat on the island, weeping and grieving and turning away Calypso's words and deceptions, longing to see his own village and the smoke rising from it. And if he had not received help from heaven, he would not have been able to return to his village."[56]

(continued on page 41)

57 | Helen of Troy, famous as "the face that launched a thousand ships and burnt the topless towers of Ilium" (Marlowe), is seen as personifying the soul. Helen has an interesting connection with Gnosticism. The church fathers Justin Martyr and Irenaeus referred to a Gnostic myth in which the first thought of God descended into the lower realms, in which she eventually became imprisoned. This is a myth that resembles the fall of Sophia (Wisdom) and the fall of the soul. This female figure endured many lives on earth, and was reincarnated as Helen of Troy. Eventually, she was reincarnated as Helene, the beloved of the semi-legendary Gnostic Simon Magus. It seems that this eventually became the story of Faust, who sold his soul in order to fulfill his desires, one of which was to see Helen of Troy.

58 | Like the biblical quotations, these extracts from Homer are paraphrases, rather than exact quotations (*The Odyssey* 4.260–61).

This reference is from *The Odyssey* 4.261–64. Perhaps the author is using an anthology of Homeric quotations (such anthologies existed and were even used for divination in a manner somewhat similar to the *I Ching*) or perhaps just quoting from memory.

59 | This reference to Aphrodite may be connected to the story of Eros or Cupid, the son of Aphrodite or Venus, and Psyche, the soul. Psyche was the youngest and most beautiful daughter of a king. Aphrodite was jealous of Psyche, and so she sent her son, Eros, to fire an arrow at her. The arrow would make Psyche fall in love with the first man that she saw (rather like the soul in *The Exegesis* who sleeps with every man who crosses her path). But Eros fell in love with Psyche when he saw her, and accidentally pricked himself with his own arrow. Eros took Psyche to his palace and made love to her in the dark every night. But Psyche could not resist bringing in a lamp one night to view her lover, and she realized that he was the god of love. Aphrodite made Psyche complete a number of tasks, the last of which involved retrieving a box from the underworld. Upon opening it, she fell asleep; Eros saw her (the roles reversed) and was reunited with her.

Again Helen said, "My heart turned itself from me. I want to return to my home."[57]

For she sighed, saying, "It is Aphrodite who deceived me and took me away from my village. I left behind my only daughter, and my good, understanding, handsome husband."[58]

For when the soul forsakes her perfect husband for the treachery of Aphrodite,[59] who exists here in the act of conception, then she will be harmed. But if she sighs and repents, she will be restored to her home.

(continued on page 43)

60 The soul's sighing and repentance is compared to the way "the people of Israel groaned under their bondage, and cried out for help, and their cry under bondage came up to God" (Exodus 2:23 RSV). Once again, the soul's escape from materiality, and her deliverance by the spirit and the father, is compared to escaping from the land of Egypt, as in *The Hymn of the Pearl*, and Abraham and Sarah's departure from Egypt.

61 Psalm 6:6–9. The Psalms contain some of the most beautiful and poignant poetry in the Hebrew Bible, or in any religious tradition. They are personal and heartfelt, concerned with the soul's longing and thirst for God. The soul is cast down and lifted up, is disquieted and comforted, fasts and waits, and awakes. All of this can be understood in terms of the fall and redemption of the soul as explained in *The Exegesis*.

62 The language of the conclusion is quite Christian. Most of the groups and individuals that we now call Gnostic did not use this as a name for themselves. Neither did they necessarily call themselves after the names of the founders of their sects. Most Gnostics thought of themselves as Christians—but they were pneumatic Christians, spiritual Christians, possessing the spirit. Their souls did not whore with thieves and adulterers, but were united with the bridegroom in the bridal chamber.

✦ "In its main lines, the story of the soul in *The Exegesis on the Soul* follows the Valentinian myth of Sophia, the last aeon who leaves the Pleroma searching for new horizons. From prostitution to repentance in tears and from repentance to her return to the house of the father, the itinerary of the soul closely recalls Sophia's journey."

—Maddalena Scopella, "Introduction to *The Exegesis on the Soul*," in *The Nag Hammadi Library in English*, edited by James Robinson, p. 190.

Surely Israel would not have been visited by God in the first place, to be brought out of the land of Egypt, brought out of the house of bondage, if it had not sighed to God and wept because of the affliction of its slavery.[60]

Once again, it is written in the Psalms, "I was troubled with my moaning. Every night I flood my bed with tears and I drench my cover with weeping. I have become old in the midst of all my enemies. Depart from me, all you workers of evil, for the lord has heard the sound of my weeping and the lord has heard my prayer."[61]

If we repent, God will listen to us, God who is long suffering and profusely merciful, to whom is glory for ever and ever. Amen![62]

(continued on page 15)

The Hymn
of the Pearl

☐ Introduction to *The Hymn of the Pearl*

The Hymn of the Pearl is a charming tale of a young prince's mission to retrieve a pearl guarded by a serpent in a faraway country. The prince forgets his mission, falls asleep, and becomes immersed in the life of the strange country, and he has to be reminded of his aim by a letter sent from his original kingdom. He then successfully takes the pearl and is rewarded with the return of his robe, and the story ends with him about to meet the king of kings. It is a story of the soul's fall and redemption, or to use Joseph Campbell's term, a hero's journey. The narrative is entirely in the first person, from the point of view of the prince, and this gives the story a greater intimacy than *The Exegesis on the Soul* and allows us to put our feet in the hero's shoes.

It has also been one of the most influential pieces of Gnostic writing, rediscovered and published in the nineteenth century long before the Nag Hammadi library was found. Almost everyone who has examined it has felt the appeal of the story, which obviously has an inner meaning but does not labor at its point. Since its modern publication, *The Hymn of the Pearl* has had a steady influence on spiritual and occult literature. The theosophist and Gnostic expert G. R. S. Mead published it in the early twentieth century with an interesting and perceptive commentary, and the great Irish poet W. B. Yeats referred to it in his elaborate mystical prose work, A Vision. It has even been adapted to music, in Gilles Gobeil's experimental work "Éclats de Perle" and in Beth the Sybil's jazz reworkings of ancient texts, among others.

The Hymn of the Pearl has come down to us as part of the Acts of Thomas, one of the apocryphal acts of the apostles. These apocryphal acts follow the adventures of the apostles after the death of Jesus, just as the canonical Acts of the Apostles covers the careers of Paul and Peter and some of the other apostles. These apocryphal acts contain extravagant stories somewhat in the style of the romances that were popular in the Hellenistic Greek literature of the time. Other surviving apocryphal acts include the also quite Gnostic Acts of John, the Acts of Philip, the Acts of Peter, and the Acts of Andrew. The Acts of Thomas survives in Greek and Syriac versions (Syriac was the dialect of Aramaic spoken in Syria). Although we possess five manuscripts of the Greek version and a massive seventy-six copies of the Syriac version, The Hymn of the Pearl is found only in one of the Greek copies and in one of the Syriac.

The Acts of Thomas follows the fortunes of the apostle (Judas) Thomas after the resurrection of Jesus. The apostles have drawn lots to determine the areas of the world that they will evangelize, and Thomas draws India as his province. Yet Thomas resists traveling to India, so the risen Christ arranges that Thomas be sold as a slave to a merchant named Habban. In the company of the merchant he travels to India. He is eventually placed in prison, where he recites The Hymn.

The Acts of Thomas is part of the Syrian Thomas tradition. Other texts that bear the name of Thomas are, of course, the Gospel of Thomas and the Book of Thomas the Contender, found in Codex II, the same volume of the Nag Hammadi texts in which the Gospel of

Thomas and *The Exegesis on the Soul* appear. Syria claims Thomas' burial place in Edessa.

Because *The Hymn of the Pearl* is found only in two copies of the Acts of Thomas—and these two versions have differences between them—it is generally (and rightly) presumed that the hymn was not originally a part of the Acts but was added later. We can be certain that *The Hymn of the Pearl* is Gnostic, but the exact variety of Gnosticism from whence it derives is disputed. The Syrian Gnostic Bardaisan (154–222 C.E.), who wrote beautiful Gnostic hymns, was once thought to be the author, but this attribution is no longer seriously considered. The extensive use of metaphor in *The Hymn* might resemble Valentinian Gnosticism, but there are no specifically Christian references in *The Hymn*, and the Valentinians were Christian Gnostics.

Most recently, a Manichaean background to *The Hymn of the Pearl* has been proposed. The Manichaeans were followers of the third-century prophet Mani, who was born in Babylon. His family background seems to have been Syrian, and eastern Syria in particular became a hotbed of Manichaeanism. Since *The Hymn* depicts Parthia as the land of the father and Egypt as the fallen world, it seems that the author's sympathies are more likely to lie in the East, which suggests that the hymn has a Manichaean origin. Egypt at that time could be considered part of the West, since it was Hellenized and part of the Roman Empire. The Parthian dynasty ended in 224 C.E., so this might suggest a cutoff date for the writing of *The Hymn*.

Islamicist Carl Ernst has recently shown that *The Hymn of the Pearl* was well known in Islam, and has survived in several languages. He includes versions in Arabic, Persian, Turkish, and Urdu.[1] There are also echoes of *The Hymn*'s theme in other Sufi literature. Thus, *The Hymn of the Pearl* was known to and used by at least three religions—Christianity (whence our versions of it in the Acts of Thomas), Gnosticism or Manichaeanism, and Islam. Few pieces of writing can claim such a widespread acceptance. Wherever and whenever it originated, *The Hymn of the Pearl* is a profound and beautiful piece of spiritual literature that speaks emotionally to readers and impresses us with the need to examine our inner lives and remind ourselves of our missions in this world.

[1] In the Acts of Thomas, the apostle Thomas recites *The Hymn of the Pearl* while he is in India. There is no reliable historical evidence that Thomas was ever actually in India, but a network of ancient Christian churches in India still bear the name Thomas, and they were probably established as the result of Syrian Christian missionaries visiting India from at least the fourth century onward. Originally, *The Hymn of the Pearl* probably had no connection with India, and was inserted into the Acts of Thomas at a convenient point. Although it originally had no connection with India, by a strange twist of history, *The Hymn of the Pearl* was translated into an Indian language Urdu from a Persian version in the nineteenth century, before it was rediscovered in the West.

[2] A text in the *Hermetica*, the pagan writings connected with the figure of Hermes Trismegistus, which were roughly contemporary with Gnosticism and which may be considered a form of pagan Gnosticism, explains, "Look at the soul of a child, my son, a soul that has not yet come to accept its separation from its source; for its body is still small and has not yet grown to its full bulk. How beautiful throughout is such a soul as that! It is not yet fouled by the bodily passions; it is still hardly detached from the soul of the Kosmos" (Corpus Hermeticum 10.15).

In spiritual literature, the innocence of children is often used to represent the uncorrupted state of the soul. But the soul cannot remain undeveloped. When the prince returns to his country and regains his robe and his status, he is an adult. In the Valentinian Gnostic text *The Interpretation of Knowledge* (Gnosis), Jesus says, "I became very small, so that through my humility I might take you up to the great height, whence you had fallen."

☐ The Hymn of the Pearl

The Hymn of the apostle Judas Thomas when he was in
the land of India:[1]

As he prayed, all the prisoners looked at him and asked
him to pray for them. And after he had prayed, he sat
down and began to recite the following psalm:—
When I was a mute child in the palace of my fathers,[2]
I rested in the wealth and luxury of those who cared
for me.

(continued on page 53)

3 "Home country" is literally *patridos*, "fatherland," emphasizing that the prince is initially at home with the Father, as is the heroine of *The Exegesis on the Soul*. The father is immediately familiar to us from Christianity, and it might be tempting to look at this in a Christian way, to see the father as God and the prince as the son of God. But in orthodox Christianity, God has a single firstborn son, Jesus, who is incarnated. In *The Hymn*, the hero is the second-born son, and the firstborn resides in Parthia with the father. Therefore, we are not expected to see the father as God and the son as Jesus in any conventional Christian sense. We do not know whether the scribe who incorporated *The Hymn* into the Acts of Thomas felt that it was Christian metaphor. We do not even know whether the scribe who added it was a Christian, a Gnostic, or a Manichaean. Although the older brother is distinct from the prince as a character, we are probably meant to see him as expressions of the same principle. The prince, the older brother, the companion, the robe, and the pearl are probably all different ways of looking at the soul, and these ancient mythical techniques help us circumvent the logical mind.

4 The sun rises in the east, and this is intended to give us the image of dawn, of the sun rising and dispelling the nighttime. *The Gospel of Truth,* one of the Gnostic texts from Nag Hammadi, equates this with gnosis, "The knowledge of the Father, they value as the dawn."

My parents equipped me and sent me from my home
    country[3] in the East.[4]
They put together a load from the riches of the treasury.
It was large, yet light enough that I could carry it by
    myself.

(*continued on page 55*)

[5] The son is given a load consisting of many treasures. Perhaps these have an allegorical meaning: Note that the gold is "from above," a detail that some scholars have concretized as meaning "from the mountains."

[6] Stephan Hoeller and others have pointed out that the treasures are arranged in descending order of worth: gold, then silver, then precious gems. The Greek word implies a ship's cargo, which would mean that the journey would be undertaken by sea. In the Greek version, he is taking pearls with him; in the Syriac, they are agates. We might wonder why the prince needs to find a pearl if he is carrying several of them with him. This may have some allegorical meaning, but it could also be an indication that the Syriac text is more original. Chalcedony is a fine form of quartz crystal. Adamant refers to any proverbially hard metal or gem.

[7] Garments are used in ancient literature to represent psychological states. A piece of clothing can be put on and taken off, just as our internal states come and go. A white robe, or a robe of light indicates an exalted state, whereas dirty clothes represent a fallen state; the sackcloth and ashes of the Bible represent a state of mourning. In another Nag Hammadi text, *The Paraphrase of Shem*, a garment of light is contrasted with a garment of fire. "Then, by the will of the Majesty, I took off my garment of light. I put on another garment of fire which has no form, which is from the mind of the power, which was separated, and which was prepared for me, according to my will, in the middle region. For the middle region covered it with a dark power in order that I might come and put it on. I went down to chaos to save the whole light from it."

This mirrors the theme of *The Hymn of the Pearl*. Scholars have referred to this as the theme of the saved savior. The savior sacrifices his divine status to let himself be caught up in the material world, and is then saved himself and makes his way back to the world of the spirit.

The load consisted of gold from above,[5] and silver from
    the great treasure-houses
and they armed me with adamant.[6]
Yet they removed my clothing,[7] which was bejeweled with
    chrysophrase, which they had made for me because
    of their love for me,
and they removed the yellow robe which was tailored
    for me.

(continued on page 57)

8 The Israelites escaped from Egypt in Exodus, and Jesus and his family went down into Egypt in Matthew, and then came back. Allegorically, Egypt is something that one enters into and yet must escape from. The material world, the physical body, or the lower self are all contenders for this. Egypt is a land where one's true identity is forgotten, where the robe of glory is exchanged for a filthy garment.

9 Perhaps the prince is intended to use his treasures to purchase the single pearl, as in the famous parable in Matthew 15:45–46 (and also the Gospel of Thomas 76), "Again, the kingdom of heaven is like a merchant in search of fine pearls, who, on finding one pearl of great value, went and sold all that he had and bought it" (RSV).

The natural pearl is produced from the excretions of the oyster, responding to the presence of an irritative such as a grain of sand. Thus, it is a symbol of something beautiful being produced from suffering. The pearl has been a staple of spiritual and religious literature, and pearls were anciently considered to be particles of light derived from the sun or the moon, just as some Gnostic and Manichaean sources view the human soul as a particle of light that should be retrieved from the world of matter.

But they made a pact with me and inscribed it in my heart
    so that I would not forget it, and they said,
Once you have gone down to Egypt,[8] if you will bring
    back the one pearl[9]

(continued on page 59)

10 The Greek word *drakōn* refers to a serpent, and it is the root of the English word dragon. The image of a dragon guarding treasure is very familiar to us from legends and from modern fantasy literature, such as *The Hobbit* by J. R. R. Tolkien.

In *The Hymn*, the serpent is obviously "evil," and his guarding of the pearl is a symptom of the fall from a higher reality. This fits in with the evil role of the serpent in the Garden of Eden in Genesis, and with the Egyptian demon Apopis, a serpent who represents chaos. Yet for some Gnostic groups, labeled as Ophites after the Greek word for serpent, *ophis*, the serpent was a positive symbol, a bringer of wisdom, and the hero of the tale of the Garden of Eden. In *On the Origin of the World*, the light of gnosis comes to Eve and her husband once she has eaten from the fruit of the tree of gnosis, offered to her by the serpent.

In the Syriac version of *The Hymn*, the serpent is located in the middle of the sea, like Leviathan, "the piercing serpent" (Isaiah 27:1), in the Hebrew Bible.

11 There are several resemblances between *The Hymn of the Pearl* and the Parable of the Prodigal Son, a parable of Jesus found only in the Gospel of Luke (Luke 14:11–32). In both, it is the younger son who leaves the land of the father and travels to a distant land, where he experiences degradation. The son's realization that his father will forgive him corresponds to the letter from the parents in *The Hymn*. In both, the triumphant return is accompanied by the gift or return of a robe. The older son in the parable is jealous of the younger son, whereas the older son in *The Hymn* is an anonymous figure. The Parable of the Prodigal Son may also be read as an allegory of the soul's fall and return.

which is there beside the devouring serpent,[10]
you will be clothed again in the jeweled garment and in
  the robe that covers it.
You will be a herald in our kingdom, with your celebrated
  brother.[11]

(continued on page 61)

12 There may be an allegorical meaning for the two guides or guardians. In his letter to the Galatians, the apostle Paul, whose writings were very popular with the Gnostics, wrote, "An heir, during the time when he is still under age, is no different from a slave, even though he is the owner of all the property; he is under the control of guardians and administrators until the time fixed by his father" (Galatians 4:1). *The Hymn of the Pearl* is the story of the soul's coming of age, a hero's journey. The stages of the narrative can be compared to our own lives. Which part of the story best encapsulates your life at this moment? Are you unsuccessfully trying to seize the pearl and about to forget your mission again, or are you trekking on the long return to the kingdom? Are you eating the food of Egypt and falling asleep, or reading the letter that calls you to awaken?

13 Scholars have also suggested that these odd little details, such as there being two guides, or of the prince meeting a compatriot in Egypt, or the specific route taken from Parthia to Egypt and back, along with the use of the first-person narrative, may indicate that the story of *The Hymn* is based on an autobiographical experience—that is, someone once went down to Egypt from Parthia and encountered some of the places, people, and events recounted in the story. It has even been suggested that this someone was the prophet Mani, who was said to be of royal blood.

14 Scholar Bentley Layton considers this "land of the Babylonians" to be not the ancient city, but a place in Egypt. The Egyptian Babylon was a fortified citadel near the great pyramids, and during the reign of the Roman emperor Augustus, a legion was stationed there. On the other hand, Mani was described as "a physician from the land of Babel," so if the Manichaean connection is intended, this may refer to the ancient city of Babylon.

So I left the East on a difficult and treacherous mission,
    with two guides[12]
because of my inexperience in traveling like this.[13]
After I had passed the region of Mosani, where there is the
    inn of the eastern merchants,
I reached the land of the Babylonians.[14]

(continued on page 63)

15 The storyteller has in mind a definite route to Egypt. Mesene, mentioned in the Syriac version, was near the mouth of the river Tigris. The location of Sarbug, also mentioned in the Syriac text, is unclear, but commentators have suggested various locations south of Babylon or on the route to Egypt.

16 The guides depart and when the hero enters Egypt he is truly alone. Perhaps this also suggests the soul's embodiment. The Gnostic scholar G. R. S. Mead has suggested that Egypt represents the body; hence, the prince entering Egypt, not his subsequent donning of dirty garments, symbolizes the soul entering the body. Perhaps the soul is being accompanied by angels when it is brought into the body. The guides depart, but the soul is never quite alone.

17 Note that the formerly mute infant has suddenly become a man. At the outset, our hero is true to his mission and lingers around the hole in which the serpent lies, watching and waiting for the moment when he might regain the pearl. But the serpent has not yet fallen asleep. It seems that it is actually impossible for the prince to succeed until he has experienced failure, which may have an important resonance in our own lives.

18 It is not clear whether the prince is a stranger to the Egyptians or to his own people. The theme of alienation is common in both Gnostic and Manichaean teaching. Hans Jonas, the notable scholar of Gnosticism, saw parallels between the Gnostics' feeling of alienation, of being a stranger in a strange land, and modern themes of alienation, which have grown since the beginning of industrialization. The Hellenization and Romanization of the Mediterranean world were accompanied by an erosion of traditional culture and religious values. Hence, Jonas related Gnostic philosophy to the modern philosophy of existentialism. The extraordinary surge of interest in Gnosticism, both in the original literature and in modern adaptations of the theme, such as the film *The Matrix*, confirms the modern relevance of these ideas.

When I entered Egypt,[15] the guides, who had been my
   fellow travelers, left me.[16]
I went immediately to the serpent and lingered at his lair,
watching carefully for it to become drowsy and to fall
   asleep, so that I could take away the pearl.[17]
Since I was alone I became as a stranger in my appearance
   and seemed foreign to my companions.[18]

(continued on page 65)

19 The fellow countryman from the East is a mysterious figure, a double to the protagonist. Perhaps he has already eaten the food of the Egyptians and fallen asleep. In that case, the fellow countryman might be the counterpart to the older brother. The older brother is the soul as it exists in the land of the father, and the fellow countryman is the soul in its fallen state in Egypt. These aspects of the story are intended to affect us indirectly, and they cannot necessarily be subjected to logical analysis.

20 The son tells his compatriot to be wary of the Egyptians and their ways. Ironically, this is the beginning of the prince's fall. Perhaps he should have been more concerned about himself than about his compatriot. Seeing the mote in his brother's eye, he fails to see the beam in his own.

21 He puts on the clothing of the Egyptians so that he will not seem foreign to them. This is his downfall, and as he adopts their clothing, he forgets his mission and purpose.

✦ "Whether this popular tale [*The Hymn*] is an old Mesopotamian legend or a Jewish or Christian story that has undergone a gnostic overlay, in the form in which it survives it is a poetic culmination of gnostic principles, conveyed with a minimum of cosmogony and deific mischief."

—Willis Barnstone and Marvin Meyer, *The Gnostic Bible*, p. 388.

But I saw my fellow countryman[19] from the East, a free
    man,
a gracious and beautiful young man, a son of nobility.
He came and accompanied me
and I spoke to him and laid hold of him,
making him a friend and companion for the journey.
I told him to guard himself against the Egyptians and
    against involvement in their impure practices.[20]
I dressed myself in their own clothing, so that I would no
    longer seem strange to them as a foreigner,[21]
so that I could retrieve the pearl, and so that the Egyptians
    would not wake the dragon against me.
But—I do not know how—they learned that I was not
    from their country.

(continued on page 67)

22 Just as clothing and nakedness can metaphorically refer to one's psychological or spiritual state, so too can being hungry and consuming food be used metaphorically. In the Greek myth of Persephone, Demeter's daughter Persephone was stolen by Hades, and lived with him in the underworld. Winter engulfed the world while Persephone was away, and Demeter traveled to the underworld to regain Persephone. However, Persephone had eaten the food of the underworld, even though it was just a single seed of pomegranate, and so she could never be wholly free of it. For this reason, it is winter for half the year while Persephone takes her place with Hades, and summer for half the year while she is free of him.

In *The Exegesis on the Soul*, a passage from Hosea in the Hebrew Bible is quoted, in which the female figure, interpreted as the soul, accepts bread and clothing from her adulterous lovers, and this accompanies her fall and degradation. In Genesis, the eating of the fruit of the Tree of the Knowledge of Good and Evil is accompanied by nakedness. Eating and drinking are ways in which our bodies relate to the physical world, and our choice of food has an effect on us. Heavy food will make us sleepy, bad food can make us nauseous, alcohol can make us drunk, herbs and medicines can cure our sicknesses. In the same way, more rarified influences, such as the things we see, the people we speak to, the books we read, can affect us. In this metaphorical form of eating, we can swallow influences that are damaging to us, or we can consume and digest spiritual teachings. The twelfth-century Persian Sufi Ruzbihan Baqli used this metaphor when he wrote, "Moses gave me the Torah to eat, Jesus gave me the Gospel to eat, David gave me the Psalm to eat, and Muhammad gave me the Koran to eat."

The Gospel of Philip 11 comments that in the Garden of Eden "people ate like the animals. But when Christ, the perfect man, came, he brought bread from heaven so that mankind might be fed with the food of man."

And they treated me with treachery and cunning, and I
tasted their food.[22]
I did not know myself any more. I did not know that I was
the son of a king, and I began to serve their king.

(continued on page 69)

23 The prince has become one of the Egyptians to such an extent that he does not even recognize the pearl when he comes across it. This is perhaps analogous to our own failure to recognize our own higher selves when they appear. The Gospel of Thomas tells us that "the kingdom of the father is already spread out on the earth and no one sees it."

24 Sleep is a metaphor for the fallen state. Some traditions would claim that this is more than metaphor, and that the difference between our usual waking state and a higher state of consciousness is greater than that between our sleep at nighttime and our usual "waking state." *The Concept of Our Great Power*, another Nag Hammadi text, tells us, "Yet you are sleeping, dreaming dreams. Wake up and return, taste and eat the true food!"

25 The prince has very quickly fallen under the influence of the Egyptians, making himself look like them, eating their food, and falling into a deep sleep. He has offered little resistance to these tricks applied to him by the Egyptians once they realized that he was not from their country.

This reminds us of the nature of the soul's journey. The prince as a child in Parthia, in the land of his father and mother, represents the soul connected to the spirit—the personal aspect of the Divine. But the soul cannot remain in this childish state—it has to grow and progress (and in that way, be of greater help to its father). The way in which it must progress takes it down, into matter, into the darkness and ignorance of the material world, where the soul is a stranger, where it eats unclean food and wears filthy and common garments in contrast to the embroidered robe that it wore at home. Yet there is a pearl in this material world, even if the soul has forgotten about it to the extent of not even noticing it. The English poet Keats commented that this world is not a vale of tears, but a vale of soul-making.

And I even came across the pearl for which I had been
  sent here by my parents.[23]
But I fell into a deep sleep[24] because of the heaviness of
  their food.[25]
My parents noticed my predicament and suffered over me.
So a proclamation was made in our kingdom, that the
  whole kingdom should meet at the gates.

(continued on page 71)

26 Yet the son, the prince, is never truly alone, and his mother and father have somehow discovered his predicament. All of the kings and nobles of Parthia, his kingdom, meet together and send out a letter. Historically, Parthia consisted of many small kingdoms, so it had a king and a king of kings.

27 The letter is from his father and mother and brother. This constitutes a trinity, and a family of a father, mother, and child is a natural way to represent three principles. In Hebrew, Aramaic, and Syriac, the spirit, *ruach*, is feminine. Thus, in the Christian trinity of father, son, and holy spirit, *ruach* once represented the family unit. But the Greek word for spirit, *pneuma*, is neuter, and the Latin *spiritus* is masculine. As the dominant language of Christianity moved from Aramaic and Hebrew to these other languages, the spirit ceased to be feminine in Christianity, although it remained feminine in Gnosticism and Manichaeanism.

28 Paul (or another author writing as Paul) quotes an otherwise unknown saying or extract from a hymn in Ephesians 5:14, "Awake, O sleeper, and arise from the dead, and Christ shall give you light."

The prince is urged to be sober. His present state is a metaphorical drunkenness, which is equivalent to the sleep that overtook the prince once he had eaten the food. Drunkenness can lend itself to two contradictory metaphorical usages. On the one hand, there is the kind of blind drunkenness that we see here, which is characterized by a lack of control, and which is a state that is lower than the state of sobriety. But on the other hand, drunkenness can be seen as an ecstatic state, which offers a higher perception of reality, hence the Sufi poems that urge us to drink wine.

And then the kings of Parthia, and those in power, and the
  leaders of the East
kept their will concerning me. That I should not be left
  alone in Egypt.[26]
The courtiers wrote to me as follows:
From your father, the king of kings, and your mother, the
  possessor of the East,[27]
and from your brother, the next in line after us, to our son
  in Egypt, peace.
Arise out of your sleep, and be sober,[28] and listen to the
  words of this letter.

(continued on page 73)

29 The soul's imprisonment in the material world is central to Gnosticism. But it is a mistake to regard pleasure alone as the main distraction of the soul. Although the soul may sometimes be lost in voluptuous excess, it is more often the petty cares and needless burdens of everyday life, the small negative emotions such as irritation, resentment, and dullness, that distract it.

30 Chrysophrase is a particular form of the gem chalcedony, green in color.

31 The book of life features in Judaism, Christianity, and Islam. The basic idea is that the names of the righteous are recorded in the book of life. Sometimes this is a kind of predestination, as in *The Hymn of the Pearl*. The name of the prince is already written in the book of life (which has been read aloud, as in a roll call), and thus he is expected to take his place in the hierarchy. In Revelation 3:5, names can be blotted out of the book of life. In the Gnostic Gospel of Truth 21, "those who are to receive the teaching [are] the living who are inscribed in the book of the living."

32 If the brother here is the older brother, then it is odd that he has been brought into the kingdom by the younger brother. This incongruity has led some scholars to suggest that it is the fellow countryman in Egypt who is figuratively being called a brother. The Syriac text simply says that the brother is already in the kingdom. If this is not just a mistake in the Greek text, then perhaps the acknowledgment that the younger son has brought the older son into the kingdom is this nonlogical way of referring to the soul as already existing in its exalted state but also having to go through the process of the fall—both being and becoming.

33 The letter has a clearly Gnostic message, and it is not addressed to the prince only but is also addressed to us: It urges us to remember our potential and possibilities, to see how we our bound up in the mundane thoughts and cares of the material world, and to remember our divine origins.

Remember that you are a son of kings. You have fallen into
    slavery.[29]
Remember your garment of chrysophrase.[30]
Remember the pearl for which you went down to Egypt.
For your name was called out in the book of life,[31]
and that too of your brother,[32] whom you brought into
    our kingdom.
And the king sealed the letter,[33] as an ambassador
because of the evil children of Babylon

(continued on page 75)

34 Scholar Bentley Layton suggests that the labyrinth referred to here is the Egyptian labyrinth, which was described by Herodotus and several later writers. In this case, the reference to the serpent might actually be to a crocodile, since Sobk the crocodile god was strongly connected with the Egyptian labyrinth. The labyrinth is long gone, but it is generally thought to have been at Hawara near Fayyum, at the temple of Amenemhet III. In its time, it was one of the most famous sites in Egypt. The best-known mythical labyrinth is the labyrinth on Crete, which held the minotaur at its center. *The Hymn* probably intends us to view the serpent in this way, or at least to resonate with the image of the labyrinth. On a psychological level, the labyrinth is us, and many traditions interpret the monster at the center of the labyrinth as the unconsciousness, or the lower self, or bodily nature, however it is expressed.

35 The content of the letter is referred to by scholars of Gnosticism as a "call." A call urges us to respond to the needs of the spirit. Not everyone receives the call, but if one does, it must be taken seriously. As the Gospel of Truth puts it, "If he has called, he hears, he answers, and he turns to him who is calling him, and ascends to him" (Gospel of Truth 21).

Gnostics did not consider that their teaching was for everyone. This is in contrast to mainstream Christianity, which feels that everyone is in need of salvation, and that this is possible for anyone who believes in Christ. Due to the relatively small number of Gnostics, they must have felt that few heard the call, and even fewer answered it. Yet some Gnostic cosmologies allowed for the whole of creation to be eventually redeemed. The letter is sealed and is thus inaccessible to those who have not heard the call. Perhaps this is a reference to the inner meaning of spiritual literature, the esoteric side, which is not accessible to those who only know of conventional religion. The contents of the letter matches what was inscribed in the prince's heart or mind before he left Parthia.

and the tyrannical demons of the labyrinth.[34]
And because of its voice and its insight, I rose up from my
sleep
and once I had received it I kissed it and read it
constantly.[35]

(continued on page 77)

36 In *The Exegesis on the Soul*, the woman's repentance and her calling to the father signal the beginning of the soul's return. Here, the
letter from Parthia represents the turnaround for the prince. These
represent two different views of this stage of the soul's evolution. From
the point of view of *The Exegesis*, the soul begins to realize its plight,
and forgiveness from a higher level enables it to move up. From the
point of view of *The Hymn*, the soul is simply lost in sleep and forget-
fulness, and it is the call from the higher level that awakens it. In both
cases, the soul returns to the father (and also to the mother in The
Hymn), so these are complementary ways of looking at the situation. In
the modern world, we are eager to take responsibility for our own
actions, but the factor of grace should never be disregarded.

37 The prince remembers everything about his origin and his mission,
and he acts immediately to take the pearl from the serpent. This time,
he is successful.

38 The son enchants the serpent using the name of his father. One's
true name is often connected with the soul in early traditions, such as
the ancient Egyptian, and much of magical practice involved invoking
gods or demons by their names. The name of God in Judaism is unpro-
nounceable and was sometimes held to have magical powers. In the
medieval Jewish satire *Toledot Yeshu*, Jesus is said to have obtained the
name of God illicitly from the temple and to have inscribed it on his
thigh so that he did not forget it when he left the temple. In *The Exegesis*, the soul calls on the name of the father when she is in her deepest distress.

And what was written there was engraved in my heart.[36]
And I remembered straight away that I was the son of kings
and my freedom was seeking my people.
And I also remembered the pearl, for which I was sent
    down to Egypt.
And I began to enchant the terrifying serpent [37]
and I tamed it by crying out the name of my father.[38]
And after I seized the pearl, I carried it away and returned
    to my parents.

(continued on page 79)

39 This dirty garment must stay in Egypt, just as the robe of glory remained in Parthia—it seems that they are mutually exclusive, and one or the other must be worn. The dirty garment may be the body, but I find it more likely that it is the lower psychological state, the soul when it is ignorant of gnosis or of the divine father and mother. On the scale of an entire lifetime, our own individual stories might resemble that of the prince—we fall into this world, we receive a call to remember our true home and real father, we remember our missions here, achieve what we are meant to do, and then return to our original kingdom. But on a day-to-day level, we are continually eating the food of the Egyptians, wearing their dirty garments, falling asleep, and forgetting our aims, then once again hearing the call and answering it.

40 The return journey is by the same route as the descent into Egypt, but the details are much more spiritualized. The prince is heading toward the light of the home country. Instead of the two guides, he is accompanied by an awakener. This awakener is a female figure, but she is not imagined as a physical companion; rather, she is more of a mystical guide, perhaps representing the soul in the form of conscience. In a parallel to the effect of the letter, she rouses him from sleep and guides him with her light and her love. As a result, he now remembers his aim, which is to regain his royal clothing. *The Hymn of the Pearl* repeats its themes using different images and characters, allowing the inner meaning to slip past the gates of our logical minds, into a deeper part of us.

41 Now that he is returning home, he passes the landmarks with ease. Babylon is on the left, traditionally the side that represented evil. This notion has survived in the English word *sinister*, which comes from the Latin word for "left."

42 The remainder of the text describes in beautiful imagery the son's exultant return to his kingdom. The son returns as a grown adult and is no longer the infant—however, he has yet to recognize fully his true self.

Once I had taken off the filthy garment[39] and left it in
    their country.
And I went off straight on the way to the light from the
    eastern fatherland.
and on the way I found my awakener,
and she roused me from sleep as if by a voice and she
    guided me with her light.
and she led me and guided me with love.[40]
I went past the labyrinth, and past Babylon on the left [41]
I reached Meson
which is the great coast
and I still could not remember my former splendor
for I was still a child and very young when I left my
    garment in my father's palace.[42]

(continued on page 81)

43 Even upon arriving in his kingdom, the prince does not recall his splendor until he sees himself, as in a mirror, and he is wearing his royal robe.

Most of us have at times experienced a state of consciousness that is beyond our familiar everyday experience. The name for it and the understanding of it varies from tradition to tradition—enlightenment, the presence of God, gnosis, a peak experience, realization, self-remembering. The description of the prince and his robe captures many aspects of this familiar yet unfamiliar state.

44 For a moment, the prince does not realize that he has changed, and we too have to recognize when we are in exalted states. One aspect of the state is that the prince knows himself—this is the immediate self-knowledge at which Gnosticism aims. This is represented too by the image of the mirror. Another aspect of this state is the feeling of being two—of being simultaneously the observer and the observed, both the robe and the prince, for which reason *The Odes of Solomon*, a collection of first- or second-century Christian psalms with strong Gnostic overtones, proclaims, "Behold, the Lord is our mirror: open the eyes and see them in him, and learn the manner of your face." Or as a Kabbalist writer puts it, "Thought is like a mirror. One looking at it sees his image inside and thinks that there are two images, but the two are really one."

45 On a light note, *The Hymn of the Pearl* has been put forward as evidence for the genuineness of the shroud of Turin. According to this interpretation—which is neither scholarly nor truly spiritual—the reason the prince sees himself in the robe is that the prince is Jesus and the robe is the shroud (with the image of Jesus marking it). Hence the later detail that the robe is embroidered with the image of the king of kings.

46 The stewards who bring the garment are also two. It is tempting to equate the two stewards with the two guides, and this is meant to parallel the theme of the prince and the robe being two in one.

But when suddenly I saw my garment reflected, as in a
   mirror,[43] I also saw my entire self in it, and I saw and
   knew myself in it,[44]
because we were made from the same substance [45]
and we were one because of our single form.
Moreover, I saw two each, not only of myself but also of
   the stewards,[46] who brought the garment,
but there was a single form for both, and a single kingly
   symbol was placed over each,
even the fine garment which was woven of bright colors,
embroidered with gold and gemstones
and pearls of an appropriate hue.

(continued on page 83)

47 The description of the robe is also more spiritualized, or more Gnostic, now that the prince is regaining it. The image of the king of kings is embroidered on the robe.

48 The robe is emitting gnosis. In the entire *Hymn*, this is the only explicit clue as to how we are meant to interpret *The Hymn*. This is in contrast to *The Exegesis on the Soul*, which constantly reminds us of the allegorical meaning of its story. The robe is gnosis, the state of the direct knowledge of God that was the aim of Gnosticism. Gnosis is the kind of knowledge that is acquired by direct insight, not by any intellectual means, and although self-knowledge may be an aspect of gnosis, it is the knowledge of God that is its principle characteristic.

49 As if our logical minds were not confused enough by the train of events, the robe itself begins to speak!

50 In the Syriac version, the robe says, "I am he who is swift in deeds, they reared me for him before my father." The Greek is different, but still not very clear. That it was inscribed by the father suggests that the robe might somehow be identified with the inscription etched into the prince's mind before the prince left for Egypt.

✦ "The soul [in *The Hymn*] is masculine, not feminine.... The important point that appears to lead to this sexual identity is that he is the heir, the child whose success and survival is most to be desired."

—Rosalie Osmond, *Imagining the Soul,* p. 41.

And the image of the king of kings was embroidered all
   over it.[47]
Gemstones were fixed together on it.
I saw again that through it impulses of gnosis were
   emitted[48]
and it was ready to speak.[49]
Then I heard it speak:
"I am the one more powerful than all men
who was inscribed by the father
and I became aware of my stature."[50]

(continued on page 85)

51 At last the prince takes the robe and is dressed in it. This is the final stage of his complete identification with the robe, and the language that describes it is mystical and allusive.

52 The brilliant colors of the robe might remind us of popular retellings of the biblical patriarch Joseph, whose long robe with sleeves in the Book of Genesis has become a coat of many colors in popular culture. Gnostics would certainly interpret Joseph's loss of his coat and its being dipped in goat's blood to suggest his death as an allegory of the descent into matter.

53 Again, the descriptions are much more symbolic now that the soul has returned home. This is not any ordinary homecoming and reuniting with one's family, but a returning to a glorious father who lives in the land of the place of peace.

✦ "[The Hymn of the Pearl] describes in allegorical form the monomyth of Gnosticism: the journey of the human spirit from the Fullness to embodiment on the earth and back to the Fullness again.... The meaning seems to be multileveled, allowing persons with various degrees of gnosis to profit from reading it."

—Stephan A. Hoeller, *Gnosticism: New Light on the Ancient Tradition of Inner Knowing*, p. 194 .

Then all the royal impulses rested on me, increasing its
    impulses.
It moved quickly from their hands
Extending itself to me.[51]
And a desire drew me to reach, to meet it and take it.
Stretching out, I was dressed in its brilliant colors,
and I clothed myself completely with my kingly robe.[52]
After clothing myself, I was taken up to the land of the
    place of peace
and bowing my head I worshipped the glory of the father,
    who sent the robe to me.[53]

(continued on page 87)

54 The prince is commended for following the directions in the letter. The two-way nature of the soul's ascent is expressed here. The prince kept the commandments, and the king kept his promise.

55 It is tempting to assume that one of the hymns being sung was *The Hymn of the Pearl*. Whether or not this was intended, this sort of alogical self-reference would fit in nicely with the techniques shown in *The Hymn of the Pearl*.

56 *The Hymn of the Pearl* ends with the prince on the threshold of the palace of the king of kings. Despite his adventures, the prince is still young. He is not yet a king, and he has no adult experience in the land of Parthia. He has not even presented the king of kings with the pearl, which is surely a tiny thing in comparison with the wealth of the palace. The story of the prince, the story of the soul, has only just begun.

57 The final lines are quite close to a beautiful Manichaean hymn from Parthia, the prince's own country:

> You shall dwell joyfully among them all for ever,
> Beside all the jewels and the venerable gods.
> Fear and death shall never overtake you,
> Neither shall destruction, distress or wretchedness.
> Peace shall be yours in the place of salvation,
> In the company of all the gods and those who dwell in peace.

Because I kept the commandments he also kept his
  promise.[54]
And I was met by his royal officials and rulers at the gates
and he delighted in me, and welcomed me to the palace.
And all his stewards were singing hymns[55] with a beautiful
  sound.
He allowed me to go to the king's doors with him,[56] so
  that with my gifts and the pearl we should appear
  together before the king.[57]

Notes □

Introduction

1. Curiously, the standard shelving category used by bookstores for the New Age section, "Mind, Body, and Spirit" precisely matches the ancient distinction of soul, body, and spirit.
2. Frazer, *The Golden Bough*, chapters 18 and 19.
3. Pyramid Text 474 in Lichtheim.
4. Xenophanes, quoted in Eliade, *The Encyclopedia of Religion*, vol. 13, p. 435.
5. *Phaedrus* 105c, trans. Jowett.
6. *Ibid.*
7. *Timaeus* 34c, trans. Jowett.
8. Eliade, *The Encyclopedia of Religion* vol. 13, p. 441
9. Descartes, quoted in MacDonald, *History of the Concept of Mind*.
10. Berkeley, *Three Dialogues Between Hylas and Philonous*, p. 233, quoted in MacDonald, *History of the Concept of Mind*, p. 340.
11. Osmond, *Imagining the Soul: A History*, p. 197.

The Exegesis on the Soul

ANNOTATIONS

14. "the soul, being reflective … purpose of his journey": Singer, *A Gnostic Book of Hours*, p. 113.
41. "The soul … all that moves besides": *Phaedrus* 245, trans. Jowett.

The Hymn of the Pearl

INTRODUCTION

1. Ernst, "Fragmentary Versions of the Apocryphal 'Hymn of the Pearl.'"

ANNOTATIONS

14. "a physician from the land of Babel": Klimheit, *Gnosis on the Silk Road*, p. 208.

44. "Thought is like a mirror ... but the two are really one": Matt, *The Essential Kabbalah*, p. 193.

57. "You shall dwell joyfully ... those who dwell in peace": Klimheit, *Gnosis on the Silk Road*, p. 114.

Suggestions for Further Reading ☐

Barnstone, Willis, and Marvin Meyer, eds. *The Gnostic Bible.* Boston: Shambhala, 2002.

Bemporad, Jack. "Soul: Jewish Concept." In *The Encyclopedia of Religion*, vol. 13, edited by Mircea Eliade. New York: Macmillan, 1987.

Bremmer, Jan. "Soul: Greek and Hellenistic Concepts." In *The Encyclopedia of Religion*, vol. 13, edited by Mircea Eliade. New York: Macmillan, 1987.

Collins, Steven. "Soul: Buddhist Concepts." In *The Encyclopedia of Religion*, vol. 13, edited by Mircea Eliade. New York: Macmillan, 1987.

Davidson, John. *The Robe of Glory: An Ancient Parable of the Soul.* Shaftesbury, Dorset, UK: Element Books, 1992.

Davies, Stevan. *The Gospel of Thomas: Annotated and Explained.* Woodstock, VT: SkyLight Paths, 2002.

———. *The Secret Book of John: Annotated and Explained.* Woodstock, VT: SkyLight Paths, 2005.

———. "Soul: Ancient Near Eastern Concepts." In *The Encyclopedia of Religion*, vol. 13, edited by Mircea Eliade. New York: Macmillan, 1987.

Eliade, Mircea, ed. *The Encyclopedia of Religion*, vol. 13. New York: Macmillan, 1987.

Eliade, Mircea, Ioan P. Couliano, and Hillary S. Wiesner. *The HarperCollins Concise Guide to World Religions.* San Francisco: HarperSanFrancisco, 1991.

Elliott, J. K. *The Apocryphal New Testament.* Oxford: Clarendon Press, 1993.

Ernst, Carl. "Fragmentary Versions of the Apocryphal 'Hymn of the Pearl ' in Arabic, Turkish, Persian, and Urdu." In *Jerusalem Studies in Arabic and Islam*, vol. 31. Jerusalem: Magnes Press, 2006.

Ferreira, Johan. *The Hymn of the Pearl: The Syriac and Greek Texts with Introduction, Translations, and Notes.* Sydney: St. Pauls, 2002.

Frazer, James. *The Golden Bough.* New York: Touchstone, 1995.

Geddes, MacGregor. "Soul: Christian Concept." In *The Encyclopedia of Religion*, vol. 13, edited by Mircea Eliade. New York: Macmillan, 1987.

Hoeller, Stephan A. *Gnosticism: New Light on the Ancient Tradition of Inner Knowing.* Wheaton, IL: Quest Books, 2002.

James, M. R. *The Apocryphal New Testament.* Oxford: Oxford University Press, 1955.

Jowett, Benjamin. *The Dialogues of Plato.* New York: Thoemmes Continuum, 1997.

Klimheit, Hans-Joachim. *Gnosis on the Silk Road: Gnostic Texts from Central Asia.* San Francisco: HarperSanFrancisco, 1993.

Layton, Bentley. *The Gnostic Scriptures: A New Translation with Annotations and Introductions.* Garden City, NY: Doubleday, 1995.

———. ed. *Nag Hammadi Codex II, 2–7*, vol 1. Leiden: Brill, 1989.

Lichtheim, M. *Ancient Egyptian Literature: A Book of Readings*, vol. 1. Berkeley: University of California Press, 1980.

MacDonald, Paul S. *History of the Concept of Mind: Speculations about Soul, Mind, and Spirit from Homer to Hume.* Aldershot, UK: Ashgate Publishing, 2003.

Mahony, William K. "Soul: Indian Concepts." In *The Encyclopedia of Religion*, vol. 13, edited by Mircea Eliade. New York: Macmillan, 1987.

Marmura, Michael E. "Soul: Islamic Concepts." In *The Encyclopedia of Religion*, vol. 13, edited by Mircea Eliade. New York: Macmillan, 1987.

Matt, Daniel C. *The Essential Kabbalah: The Heart of Jewish Mysticism.* San Francisco: HarperSanFrancisco, 1996.

Mead, G. R. S. *Echoes from the Gnosis: Centennial Edition.* Wheaton, IL: Quest Books, 2006.

Nash, John. *The Quest for the Soul: The Age-Old Search for Our Inner Spiritual Nature.* Bloomington, IN: Authorhouse, 2004.

Novak, Peter. *The Division of Consciousness: The Secret Afterlife of the Human Psyche.* Charlottesville, VA: Hampton Roads Publishing, 1997.

Osmond, Rosalie. *Imagining the Soul: A History.* Stroud, UK: Sutton Publishing, 2004.

Price, Robert M. *Deconstructing Jesus.* Amherst, NY: Prometheus, 2000.

Rivière, Claude. "Soul: Concepts in Primitive Religions." In *The Encyclopedia of Religion*, vol. 13, edited by Mircea Eliade. New York: Macmillan, 1987.

Robinson, James, ed. *The Nag Hammadi Library in English*, rev. ed. San Francisco: Harper and Row, 1988.

Robson, James. *Christ in Islam.* Oregon House, CA: Bardic Press, 2006.

Salaman, Clement, Dorine van Oyen, William D. Wharton, and Jean-Pierre Mahé. *The Way of Hermes: New Translations of* The Corpus Hermeticum *and* The Definitions of Hermes Trismegistus to Asclepius. Rochester, VT: Inner Traditions, 2004.

Schneemelcher, Wilhelm, ed., Wilson, R. McL., trans. *New Testament Apocrypha, Vol. 2: Writings Relating to the Apostles, Apocalypses, and Related Subjects*, rev. ed. Louisville, KY: Westminster/John Knox Press, 1991.

Scholem, Gershom G. *Major Trends in Jewish Mysticism.* New York: Schocken Books, 1961.

Singer, June. *A Gnostic Book of Hours: Keys to Inner Wisdom.* Berwick, ME: Nicolas-Hays, 2003.

Smith, Andrew Phillip. *The Gospel of Philip: Annotated and Explained.* Woodstock, VT: SkyLight Paths, 2005.

———. *The Gospel of Thomas: A New Version Based on Its Inner Meaning.* Oregon House, CA: Ulysses Books, 2002.

Thomas, R. S. *Collected Poems, 1945–1990.* Sheffield: Phoenix Press, 2000.

Wei-Ming, Tu. "Soul: Chinese Concepts." In *The Encyclopedia of Religion*, vol. 13, edited by Mircea Eliade. New York: Macmillan, 1987.

Global Spiritual Perspectives

Spiritual Perspectives on America's Role as Superpower
by the Editors at SkyLight Paths
Are we the world's good neighbor or a global bully? From a spiritual perspective, what are America's responsibilities as the only remaining superpower? Contributors:
Dr. Beatrice Bruteau • Dr. Joan Brown Campbell • Tony Campolo • Rev. Forrest Church • Lama Surya Das • Matthew Fox • Kabir Helminski • Thich Nhat Hanh • Eboo Patel • Abbot M. Basil Pennington, ocso • Dennis Prager • Rosemary Radford Ruether • Wayne Teasdale • Rev. William McD. Tully • Rabbi Arthur Waskow • John Wilson
5½ x 8½, 256 pp, Quality PB, 978-1-893361-81-2 **$16.95**

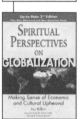

Spiritual Perspectives on Globalization, 2nd Edition
Making Sense of Economic and Cultural Upheaval
by Ira Rifkin; Foreword by Dr. David Little, Harvard Divinity School
What is globalization? Surveys the religious landscape. Includes a new Discussion Guide designed for group use.
5½ x 8½, 256 pp, Quality PB, 978-1-59473-045-0 **$16.99**

Hinduism / Vedanta

The Four Yogas
A Guide to the Spiritual Paths of Action, Devotion, Meditation and Knowledge
by Swami Adiswarananda 6 x 9, 320 pp, HC, 978-1-59473-143-3 **$29.99**

Meditation & Its Practices
A Definitive Guide to Techniques and Traditions of Meditation in Yoga and Vedanta
by Swami Adiswarananda 6 x 9, 504 pp, Quality PB, 978-1-59473-105-1 **$19.99**

The Spiritual Quest and the Way of Yoga: The Goal, the Journey and the Milestones
by Swami Adiswarananda 6 x 9, 288 pp, HC, 978-1-59473-113-6 **$29.99**

Sri Ramakrishna, the Face of Silence
by Swami Nikhilananda and Dhan Gopal Mukerji
Edited with an Introduction by Swami Adiswarananda; Foreword by Dhan Gopal Mukerji II
Classic biographies present the life and thought of Sri Ramakrishna.
6 x 9, 352 pp, HC, 978-1-59473-115-0 **$29.99**

Sri Sarada Devi, The Holy Mother
Her Teachings and Conversations
Translated with Notes by Swami Nikhilananda; Edited with an Introduction by Swami Adiswarananda
6 x 9, 288 pp, HC, 978-1-59473-070-2 **$29.99**

The Vedanta Way to Peace and Happiness by Swami Adiswarananda
6 x 9, 240 pp, HC, 978-1-59473-034-4 **$29.99**

Vivekananda, World Teacher: His Teachings on the Spiritual Unity of Humankind
Edited and with an Introduction by Swami Adiswarananda
6 x 9, 272 pp, Quality PB, 978-1-59473-210-2 **$21.99**

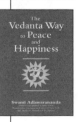

Sikhism

The First Sikh Spiritual Master
Timeless Wisdom from the Life and Teachings of Guru Nanak by Harish Dhillon
Tells the story of a unique spiritual leader who showed a gentle, peaceful path to God-realization while highlighting Guru Nanak's quest for tolerance and compassion. 6 x 9, 192 pp, Quality PB, 978-1-59473-209-6 **$16.99**

Or phone, fax, mail or e-mail to: SKYLIGHT PATHS Publishing
Sunset Farm Offices, Route 4 • P.O. Box 237 • Woodstock, Vermont 05091
Tel: (802) 457-4000 • Fax: (802) 457-4004 • www.skylightpaths.com
Credit card orders: (800) 962-4544 (8:30AM–5:30PM ET Monday–Friday)
Generous discounts on quantity orders. SATISFACTION GUARANTEED. Prices subject to change.

Midrash Fiction / Folktales

Abraham's Bind & Other Bible Tales of Trickery, Folly, Mercy and Love by Michael J. Caduto

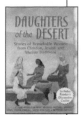

New retellings of episodes in the lives of familiar biblical characters explore relevant life lessons.

6 x 9, 224 pp, HC, 978-1-59473-186-0 **$19.99**

Daughters of the Desert: Stories of Remarkable Women from Christian, Jewish and Muslim Traditions by Claire Rudolf Murphy, Meghan Nuttall Sayres, Mary Cronk Farrell, Sarah Conover and Betsy Wharton

Breathes new life into the old tales of our female ancestors in faith. Uses traditional scriptural passages as starting points, then with vivid detail fills in historical context and place. Chapters reveal the voices of Sarah, Hagar, Huldah, Esther, Salome, Mary Magdalene, Lydia, Khadija, Fatima and many more. Historical fiction ideal for readers of all ages. Quality paperback includes reader's discussion guide.

5½ x 8½, 192 pp, Quality PB, 978-1-59473-106-8 **$14.99**
HC, 192 pp, 978-1-893361-72-0 **$19.95**

The Triumph of Eve & Other Subversive Bible Tales
by Matt Biers-Ariel

Many people were taught and remember only a one-dimensional Bible. These engaging retellings are the antidote to this—they're witty, often hilarious, always profound, and invite you to grapple with questions and issues that are often hidden in the original text.

5½ x 8½, 192 pp, Quality PB, 978-1-59473-176-1 **$14.99**
HC, 192 pp, 978-1-59473-040-5 **$19.99**

Also avail.: **The Triumph of Eve Teacher's Guide**
8½ x 11, 44 pp, PB, 978-1-59473-152-5 **$0.99**

Wisdom in the Telling
Finding Inspiration and Grace in Traditional Folktales and Myths Retold
by Lorraine Hartin-Gelardi

6 x 9, 224 pp, HC, 978-1-59473-185-3 **$19.99**

Religious Etiquette / Reference

How to Be a Perfect Stranger, 4th Edition: The Essential Religious Etiquette Handbook Edited by Stuart M. Matlins and Arthur J. Magida

The indispensable guidebook to help the well-meaning guest when visiting other people's religious ceremonies. A straightforward guide to the rituals and celebrations of the major religions and denominations in the United States and Canada from the perspective of an interested guest of any other faith, based on information obtained from authorities of each religion. Belongs in every living room, library and office. Covers:

African American Methodist Churches • Assemblies of God • Bahá'í • Baptist • Buddhist • Christian Church (Disciples of Christ) • Christian Science (Church of Christ, Scientist) • Churches of Christ • Episcopalian and Anglican • Hindu • Islam • Jehovah's Witnesses • Jewish • Lutheran • Mennonite/Amish • Methodist • Mormon (Church of Jesus Christ of Latter-day Saints) • Native American/First Nations • Orthodox Churches • Pentecostal Church of God • Presbyterian • Quaker (Religious Society of Friends) • Reformed Church in America/Canada • Roman Catholic • Seventh-day Adventist • Sikh • Unitarian Universalist • United Church of Canada • United Church of Christ

6 x 9, 432 pp, Quality PB, 978-1-59473-140-2 **$19.99**

The Perfect Stranger's Guide to Funerals and Grieving Practices: A Guide to Etiquette in Other People's Religious Ceremonies Edited by Stuart M. Matlins

6 x 9, 240 pp, Quality PB, 978-1-893361-20-1 **$16.95**

The Perfect Stranger's Guide to Wedding Ceremonies: A Guide to Etiquette in Other People's Religious Ceremonies Edited by Stuart M. Matlins

6 x 9, 208 pp, Quality PB, 978-1-893361-19-5 **$16.95**

Meditation / Prayer

Prayers to an Evolutionary God
by William Cleary; Afterword by Diarmuid O'Murchu
How is it possible to pray when God is dislocated from heaven, dispersed all around us, and more of a creative force than an all-knowing father? Inspired by the spiritual and scientific teachings of Diarmuid O'Murchu and Teilhard de Chardin, Cleary reveals that religion and science can be combined to create an expanding view of the universe—an evolutionary faith.
6 x 9, 208 pp, HC, 978-1-59473-006-1 **$21.99**

Psalms: A Spiritual Commentary
by M. Basil Pennington, ocso; Illustrations by Phillip Ratner
Showing how the Psalms give profound and candid expression to both our highest aspirations and our deepest pain, the late, highly respected Cistercian Abbot M. Basil Pennington shares his reflections on some of the most beloved passages from the Bible's most widely read book.
6 x 9, 176 pp, HC, 24 full-page b/w illus., 978-1-59473-141-9 **$19.99**

The Song of Songs: A Spiritual Commentary
by M. Basil Pennington, ocso; Illustrations by Phillip Ratner
Join the late M. Basil Pennington as he ruminates on the Bible's most challenging mystical text. Follow a path into the Songs that weaves through his inspired words and the evocative drawings of Jewish artist Phillip Ratner—a path that reveals your own humanity and leads to the deepest delight of your soul.
6 x 9, 160 pp, HC, 14 b/w illus., 978-1-59473-004-7 **$19.99**

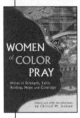

Women of Color Pray: Voices of Strength, Faith, Healing, Hope and Courage *Edited and with Introductions by Christal M. Jackson*
Through these prayers, poetry, lyrics, meditations and affirmations, you will share in the strong and undeniable connection women of color share with God. It will challenge you to explore new ways of prayerful expression.
5 x 7¼, 208 pp, Quality PB, 978-1-59473-077-1 **$15.99**

The Art of Public Prayer: Not for Clergy Only
by Lawrence A. Hoffman
An ecumenical resource for all people looking to change hardened worship patterns.
6 x 9, 288 pp, Quality PB, 978-1-893361-06-5 **$18.99**

Finding Grace at the Center, 3rd Ed.: The Beginning of Centering Prayer
by M. Basil Pennington, ocso, Thomas Keating, ocso, and Thomas E. Clarke, sj
Foreword by Rev. Cynthia Bourgeault, PhD
5 x 7¼, 128 pp, Quality PB, 978-1-59473-182-2 **$12.99**

A Heart of Stillness: A Complete Guide to Learning the Art of Meditation
by David A. Cooper 5½ x 8½, 272 pp, Quality PB, 978-1-59473-03-4 **$16.95**

Meditation without Gurus: A Guide to the Heart of Practice
by Clark Strand 5½ x 8½, 192 pp, Quality PB, 978-1-893361-93-5 **$16.95**

Praying with Our Hands: 21 Practices of Embodied Prayer from the World's
Spiritual Traditions *by Jon M. Sweeney; Photographs by Jennifer J. Wilson; Foreword by Mother Tessa Bielecki; Afterword by Taitetsu Unno, PhD*
8 x 8, 96 pp, 22 duotone photos, Quality PB, 978-1-893361-16-4 **$16.95**

Silence, Simplicity & Solitude: A Complete Guide to Spiritual Retreat at Home
by David A. Cooper 5½ x 8½, 336 pp, Quality PB, 978-1-893361-04-1 **$16.95**

Three Gates to Meditation Practice: A Personal Journey into Sufism, Buddhism, and Judaism *by David A. Cooper* 5½ x 8½, 240 pp, Quality PB, 978-1-893361-22-5 **$16.95**

Women Pray: Voices through the Ages, from Many Faiths, Cultures and Traditions
Edited and with Introductions by Monica Furlong
5 x 7¼, 256 pp, Quality PB, 978-1-59473-071-9 **$15.99**
Deluxe HC with ribbon marker, 978-1-893361-25-6 **$19.95**

Kabbalah from Jewish Lights Publishing

Awakening to Kabbalah: The Guiding Light of Spiritual Fulfillment
by Rav Michael Laitman, PhD 6 x 9, 192 pp, HC, 978-1-58023-264-7 **$21.99**

Cast in God's Image: Discover Your Personality Type Using the Enneagram and Kabbalah
by Rabbi Howard A. Addison 7 x 9, 176 pp, Quality PB, 978-1-58023-124-4 **$16.95**

Ehyeh: A Kabbalah for Tomorrow *by Dr. Arthur Green*
6 x 9, 224 pp, Quality PB, 978-1-58023-213-5 **$16.99**

The Enneagram and Kabbalah, 2nd Edition: Reading Your Soul
by Rabbi Howard A. Addison 6 x 9, 192 pp, Quality PB, 978-1-58023-229-6 **$16.99**

Finding Joy: A Practical Spiritual Guide to Happiness *by Dannel I. Schwartz with Mark Hass*
6 x 9, 192 pp, Quality PB, 978-1-58023-009-4 **$14.95**

The Gift of Kabbalah: Discovering the Secrets of Heaven, Renewing Your Life on Earth
by Tamar Frankiel, PhD 6 x 9, 256 pp, Quality PB, 978-1-58023-141-1 **$16.95**
HC, 978-1-58023-108-4 **$21.95**

Honey from the Rock: An Easy Introduction to Jewish Mysticism
by Lawrence Kushner 6 x 9, 176 pp, Quality PB, 978-1-58023-073-5 **$16.95**

Kabbalah: A Brief Introduction for Christians
by Tamar Frankiel, PhD 5½ x 8½, 176 pp, Quality PB, 978-1-58023-303-3 **$16.99**

Zohar: Annotated & Explained *Translation and Annotation by Dr. Daniel C. Matt*
Foreword by Andrew Harvey 5½ x 8½, 176 pp, Quality PB, 978-1-893361-51-5 **$15.99**

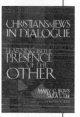

Judaism / Christianity

Christians and Jews in Dialogue: Learning in the Presence of the Other
by Mary C. Boys and Sara S. Lee; Foreword by Dorothy C. Bass
Inspires renewed commitment to dialogue between religious traditions and illuminates how it should happen. Explains the transformative work of creating environments for Jews and Christians to study together and enter the dynamism of the other's religious tradition.
6 x 9, 240 pp, HC, 978-1-59473-144-0 **$21.99**

Healing the Jewish-Christian Rift: Growing Beyond Our Wounded History
by Ron Miller and Laura Bernstein; Foreword by Dr. Beatrice Bruteau
6 x 9, 288 pp, Quality PB, 978-1-59473-139-6 **$18.99**

Introducing My Faith and My Community
The Jewish Outreach Institute Guide for the Christian in a Jewish Interfaith Relationship
by Rabbi Kerry M. Olitzky 6 x 9, 176 pp, Quality PB, 978-1-58023-192-3 **$16.99** *(a Jewish Lights book)*

The Jewish Approach to God: A Brief Introduction for Christians
by Rabbi Neil Gillman 5½ x 8½, 192 pp, Quality PB, 978-1-58023-190-9 **$16.95** *(a Jewish Lights book)*

Jewish Holidays: A Brief Introduction for Christians
by Rabbi Kerry M. Olitzky and Rabbi Daniel Judson
5½ x 8½, 176 pp, Quality PB, 978-1-58023-302-6 **$16.99** *(a Jewish Lights book)*

Jewish Ritual: A Brief Introduction for Christians
by Rabbi Kerry M. Olitzky and Rabbi Daniel Judson
5½ x 8½, 144 pp, Quality PB, 978-1-58023-210-4 **$14.99** *(a Jewish Lights book)*

Jewish Spirituality: A Brief Introduction for Christians
by Rabbi Lawrence Kushner
5½ x 8½, 112 pp, Quality PB, 978-1-58023-150-3 **$12.95** *(a Jewish Lights book)*

A Jewish Understanding of the New Testament
by Rabbi Samuel Sandmel; new Preface by Rabbi David Sandmel
5½ x 8½, 368 pp, Quality PB, 978-1-59473-048-1 **$19.99**

We Jews and Jesus
Exploring Theological Differences for Mutual Understanding
by Rabbi Samuel Sandmel; new Preface by Rabbi David Sandmel A Classic Reprint
Written in a non-technical way for the layperson, this candid and forthright look at the what and why of the Jewish attitude toward Jesus is a clear and forceful exposition that guides both Christians and Jews in relevant discussion.
6 x 9, 192 pp, Quality PB, 978-1-59473-208-9 **$16.99**

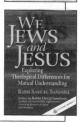

Sacred Texts—SkyLight Illuminations Series

Offers today's spiritual seeker an accessible entry into the great classic texts of the world's spiritual traditions. Each classic is presented in an accessible translation, with facing pages of guided commentary from experts, giving you the keys you need to understand the history, context and meaning of the text. This series enables you, whatever your background, to experience and understand classic spiritual texts directly, and to make them a part of your life.

CHRISTIANITY

The End of Days: Essential Selections from Apocalyptic Texts— Annotated & Explained *Annotation by Robert G. Clouse*
Helps you understand the complex Christian visions of the end of the world.
5½ x 8½, 224 pp, Quality PB, 978-1-59473-170-9 **$16.99**

The Hidden Gospel of Matthew: Annotated & Explained
Translation & Annotation by Ron Miller
Takes you deep into the text cherished around the world to discover the words and events that have the strongest connection to the historical Jesus.
5½ x 8½, 272 pp, Quality PB, 978-1-59473-038-2 **$16.99**

The Lost Sayings of Jesus: Teachings from Ancient Christian, Jewish, Gnostic and Islamic Sources—Annotated & Explained
Translation & Annotation by Andrew Phillip Smith; Foreword by Stephan A. Hoeller
This collection of more than three hundred sayings depicts Jesus as a Wisdom teacher who speaks to people of all faiths as a mystic and spiritual master.
5½ x 8½, 240 pp, Quality PB, 978-1-59473-172-3 **$16.99**

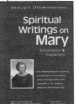

Philokalia: The Eastern Christian Spiritual Texts—Selections Annotated & Explained *Annotation by Allyne Smith; Translation by G. E. H. Palmer, Phillip Sherrard and Bishop Kallistos Ware*
The first approachable introduction to the wisdom of the Philokalia, which is the classic text of Eastern Christian spirituality.
5½ x 8½, 240 pp, Quality PB, 978-1-59473-103-7 **$16.99**

Spiritual Writings on Mary: Annotated & Explained
Annotation by Mary Ford-Grabowsky; Foreword by Andrew Harvey
Examines the role of Mary, the mother of Jesus, as a source of inspiration in history and in life today. 5½ x 8½, 288 pp, Quality PB, 978-1-59473-001-6 **$16.99**

The Way of a Pilgrim: Annotated & Explained
Translation & Annotation by Gleb Pokrovsky; Foreword by Andrew Harvey
This classic of Russian spirituality is the delightful account of one man who sets out to learn the prayer of the heart, also known as the "Jesus prayer."
5½ x 8½, 160 pp, Illus., Quality PB, 978-1-893361-31-7 **$14.95**

MORMONISM

The Book of Mormon: Selections Annotated & Explained
Annotation by Jana Riess; Foreword by Phyllis Tickle
Explores the sacred epic that is cherished by more than twelve million members of the LDS church as the keystone of their faith.
5½ x 8½, 272 pp, Quality PB, 978-1-59473-076-4 **$16.99**

NATIVE AMERICAN

Native American Stories of the Sacred: Annotated & Explained
Retold & Annotated by Evan T. Pritchard
Intended for more than entertainment, these teaching tales contain elegantly simple illustrations of time-honored truths.
5½ x 8½, 272 pp, Quality PB, 978-1-59473-112-9 **$16.99**

Sacred Texts—cont.

GNOSTICISM

The Gospel of Philip: Annotated & Explained
Translation & Annotation by Andrew Phillip Smith; Foreword by Stevan Davies
Reveals otherwise unrecorded sayings of Jesus and fragments of Gnostic mythology.
5½ x 8½, 160 pp, Quality PB, 978-1-59473-111-2 **$16.99**

The Gospel of Thomas: Annotated & Explained
Translation & Annotation by Stevan Davies Sheds new light on the origins of Christianity and portrays Jesus as a wisdom-loving sage. 5½ x 8½, 192 pp, Quality PB, 978-1-893361-45-4 **$16.99**

The Secret Book of John: The Gnostic Gospel—Annotated & Explained
Translation & Annotation by Stevan Davies The most significant and influential text of the ancient Gnostic religion. 5½ x 8½, 208 pp, Quality PB, 978-1-59473-082-5 **$16.99**

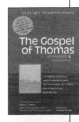

JUDAISM

The Divine Feminine in Biblical Wisdom Literature
Selections Annotated & Explained
Translation & Annotation by Rabbi Rami Shapiro; Foreword by Rev. Cynthia Bourgeault, PhD
Uses the Hebrew books of Psalms, Proverbs, Song of Songs, Ecclesiastes and Job, Wisdom literature and the Wisdom of Solomon to clarify who Wisdom is.
5½ x 8½, 240 pp, Quality PB, 978-1-59473-109-9 **$16.99**

Ethics of the Sages: *Pirke Avot*—Annotated & Explained
Translation & Annotation by Rabbi Rami Shapiro Clarifies the ethical teachings of the early Rabbis. 5½ x 8½, 192 pp, Quality PB, 978-1-59473-207-2 **$16.99**

Hasidic Tales: Annotated & Explained
Translation & Annotation by Rabbi Rami Shapiro
Introduces the legendary tales of the impassioned Hasidic rabbis, presenting them as stories rather than as parables. 5½ x 8½, 240 pp, Quality PB, 978-1-893361-86-7 **$16.95**

The Hebrew Prophets: Selections Annotated & Explained
Translation & Annotation by Rabbi Rami Shapiro; Foreword by Zalman M. Schachter-Shalomi
Focuses on the central themes covered by all the Hebrew prophets.
5½ x 8½, 224 pp, Quality PB, 978-1-59473-037-5 **$16.99**

Zohar: Annotated & Explained *Translation & Annotation by Daniel C. Matt*
The best-selling author of *The Essential Kabbalah* brings together in one place the most important teachings of the Zohar, the canonical text of Jewish mystical tradition.
5½ x 8½, 176 pp, Quality PB, 978-1-893361-51-5 **$15.99**

EASTERN RELIGIONS

Bhagavad Gita: Annotated & Explained *Translation by Shri Purohit Swami*
Annotation by Kendra Crossen Burroughs Explains references and philosophical terms, shares the interpretations of famous spiritual leaders and scholars, and more.
5½ x 8½, 192 pp, Quality PB, 978-1-893361-28-7 **$16.95**

Dhammapada: Annotated & Explained *Translation by Max Müller and revised by Jack Maguire; Annotation by Jack Maguire* Contains all of Buddhism's key teachings.
5½ x 8½, 160 pp, b/w photos, Quality PB, 978-1-893361-42-3 **$14.95**

Rumi and Islam: Selections from His Stories, Poems, and Discourses—
Annotated & Explained *Translation & Annotation by Ibrahim Gamard*
Focuses on Rumi's place within the Sufi tradition of Islam, providing insight into the mystical side of the religion. 5½ x 8½, 240 pp, Quality PB, 978-1-59473-002-3 **$15.99**

Selections from the Gospel of Sri Ramakrishna: Annotated & Explained
Translation by Swami Nikhilananda; Annotation by Kendra Crossen Burroughs
Introduces the fascinating world of the Indian mystic and the universal appeal of his message. 5½ x 8½, 240 pp, b/w photos, Quality PB, 978-1-893361-46-1 **$16.95**

Tao Te Ching: Annotated & Explained *Translation & Annotation by Derek Lin*
Foreword by Lama Surya Das Introduces an Eastern classic in an accessible, poetic and completely original way. 5½ x 8½, 192 pp, Quality PB, 978-1-59473-204-1 **$16.99**

Spirituality of the Seasons

Autumn: A Spiritual Biography of the Season
Edited by Gary Schmidt and Susan M. Felch; Illustrations by Mary Azarian
Rejoice in autumn as a time of preparation and reflection. Includes Wendell Berry, David James Duncan, Robert Frost, A. Bartlett Giamatti, E. B. White, P. D. James, Julian of Norwich, Garret Keizer, Tracy Kidder, Anne Lamott, May Sarton.
6 x 9, 320 pp, 5 b/w illus., Quality PB, 978-1-59473-118-1 **$18.99**
HC, 978-1-59473-005-4 **$22.99**

Spring: A Spiritual Biography of the Season
Edited by Gary Schmidt and Susan M. Felch; Illustrations by Mary Azarian
Explore the gentle unfurling of spring and reflect on how nature celebrates rebirth and renewal. Includes Jane Kenyon, Lucy Larcom, Harry Thurston, Nathaniel Hawthorne, Noel Perrin, Annie Dillard, Martha Ballard, Barbara Kingsolver, Dorothy Wordsworth, Donald Hall, David Brill, Lionel Basney, Isak Dinesen, Paul Laurence Dunbar.
6 x 9, 352 pp, 6 b/w illus., HC, 978-1-59473-114-3 **$21.99**

Summer: A Spiritual Biography of the Season
Edited by Gary Schmidt and Susan M. Felch; Illustrations by Barry Moser
"A sumptuous banquet.... These selections lift up an exquisite wholeness found within an everyday sophistication."— ★ *Publishers Weekly* starred review
Includes Anne Lamott, Luci Shaw, Ray Bradbury, Richard Selzer, Thomas Lynch, Walt Whitman, Carl Sandburg, Sherman Alexie, Madeleine L'Engle, Jamaica Kincaid.
6 x 9, 304 pp, 5 b/w illus., HC, 978-1-59473-083-2 **$21.99**

Winter: A Spiritual Biography of the Season
Edited by Gary Schmidt and Susan M. Felch; Illustrations by Barry Moser
"This outstanding anthology features top-flight nature and spirituality writers on the fierce, inexorable season of winter.... Remarkably lively and warm, despite the icy subject." — ★ *Publishers Weekly* starred review.
Includes Will Campbell, Rachel Carson, Annie Dillard, Donald Hall, Ron Hansen, Jane Kenyon, Jamaica Kincaid, Barry Lopez, Kathleen Norris, John Updike, E. B. White.
6 x 9, 288 pp, 6 b/w illus., Deluxe PB w/flaps, 978-1-893361-92-8 **$18.95**
HC, 978-1-893361-53-9 **$21.95**

Spirituality / Animal Companions

Blessing the Animals: Prayers and Ceremonies to Celebrate God's Creatures, Wild and Tame *Edited by Lynn L. Caruso* 5 x 7¼, 256 pp, HC, 978-1-59473-145-7 **$19.99**

What Animals Can Teach Us about Spirituality: Inspiring Lessons from Wild and Tame Creatures *by Diana L. Guerrero* 6 x 9, 176 pp, Quality PB, 978-1-893361-84-3 **$16.95**

Spirituality

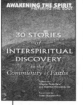

Awakening the Spirit, Inspiring the Soul
30 Stories of Interspiritual Discovery in the Community of Faiths
Edited by Brother Wayne Teasdale and Martha Howard, MD; Foreword by Joan Borysenko, PhD
Thirty original spiritual mini-autobiographies showcase the varied ways that people come to faith—and what that means—in today's multi-religious world.
6 x 9, 224 pp, HC, 978-1-59473-039-9 **$21.99**

The Alphabet of Paradise: An A–Z of Spirituality for Everyday Life
by Howard Cooper 5 x 7¼, 224 pp, Quality PB, 978-1-893361-80-5 **$16.95**

Creating a Spiritual Retirement: A Guide to the Unseen Possibilities in Our Lives
by Molly Srode 6 x 9, 208 pp, b/w photos, Quality PB, 978-1-59473-050-4 **$14.99**
HC, 978-1-893361-75-1 **$19.95**

Finding Hope: Cultivating God's Gift of a Hopeful Spirit
by Marcia Ford 8 x 8, 200 pp, Quality PB, 978-1-59473-211-9 **$16.99**

The Geography of Faith: Underground Conversations on Religious, Political and Social Change *by Daniel Berrigan and Robert Coles* 6 x 9, 224 pp, Quality PB, 978-1-893361-40-5 **$16.95**

God Within: Our Spiritual Future—As Told by Today's New Adults *Edited by Jon M. Sweeney and the Editors at SkyLight Paths* 6 x 9, 176 pp, Quality PB, 978-1-893361-15-7 **$14.95**

Spirituality & Crafts

The Knitting Way: A Guide to Spiritual Self-Discovery
by Linda Skolnik and Janice MacDaniels
7 x 9, 240 pp, Quality PB, 978-1-59473-079-5 **$16.99**

The Quilting Path
A Guide to Spiritual Discovery through Fabric, Thread and Kabbalah
by Louise Silk
7 x 9, 192 pp, Quality PB, 978-1-59473-206-5 **$16.99**

Spiritual Practice

Divining the Body
Reclaim the Holiness of Your Physical Self *by Jan Phillips*
A practical and inspiring guidebook for connecting the body and soul in spiritual practice. Leads you into a milieu of reverence, mystery and delight, helping you discover your body as a pathway to the Divine.
8 x 8, 256 pp, Quality PB, 978-1-59473-080-1 **$16.99**

Finding Time for the Timeless: Spirituality in the Workweek
by John McQuiston II
Simple, refreshing stories that provide you with examples of how you can refocus and enrich your daily life using prayer or meditation, ritual and other forms of spiritual practice. 5½ x 6¾, 208 pp, HC, 978-1-59473-035-1 **$17.99**

The Gospel of Thomas
A Guidebook for Spiritual Practice *by Ron Miller; Translations by Stevan Davies*
An innovative guide to bring a new spiritual classic into daily life.
6 x 9, 160 pp, Quality PB, 978-1-59473-047-4 **$14.99**

Earth, Water, Fire, and Air: Essential Ways of Connecting to Spirit
by Cait Johnson 6 x 9, 224 pp, HC, 978-1-893361-65-2 **$19.95**

Labyrinths from the Outside In: Walking to Spiritual Insight—A Beginner's Guide
by Donna Schaper and Carole Ann Camp
6 x 9, 208 pp, b/w illus. and photos, Quality PB, 978-1-893361-18-8 **$16.95**

Practicing the Sacred Art of Listening: A Guide to Enrich Your Relationships and Kindle Your Spiritual Life—The Listening Center Workshop
by Kay Lindahl 8 x 8, 176 pp, Quality PB, 978-1-893361-85-0 **$16.95**

Releasing the Creative Spirit: Unleash the Creativity in Your Life
by Dan Wakefield 7 x 10, 256 pp, Quality PB, 978-1-893361-36-2 **$16.95**

The Sacred Art of Bowing: Preparing to Practice
by Andi Young 5½ x 8½, 128 pp, b/w illus., Quality PB, 978-1-893361-82-9 **$14.95**

The Sacred Art of Chant: Preparing to Practice
by Ana Hernández 5½ x 8½, 192 pp, Quality PB, 978-1-59473-036-8 **$15.99**

The Sacred Art of Fasting: Preparing to Practice
by Thomas Ryan, CSP 5½ x 8½, 192 pp, Quality PB, 978-1-59473-078-8 **$15.99**

The Sacred Art of Forgiveness: Forgiving Ourselves and Others through God's Grace
by Marcia Ford 8 x 8, 176 pp, Quality PB, 978-1-59473-175-4 **$16.99**

The Sacred Art of Listening: Forty Reflections for Cultivating a Spiritual Practice
by Kay Lindahl; Illustrations by Amy Schnapper
8 x 8, 160 pp, b/w illus., Quality PB, 978-1-893361-44-7 **$16.99**

The Sacred Art of Lovingkindness: Preparing to Practice
by Rabbi Rami Shapiro; Foreword by Marcia Ford
5½ x 8½, 176 pp, Quality PB, 978-1-59473-151-8 **$16.99**

Sacred Speech: A Practical Guide for Keeping Spirit in Your Speech
by Rev. Donna Schaper 6 x 9, 176 pp, Quality PB, 978-1-59473-068-9 **$15.99**
HC, 978-1-893361-74-4 **$21.95**

About SKYLIGHT PATHS Publishing

SkyLight Paths Publishing is creating a place where people of different spiritual traditions come together for challenge and inspiration, a place where we can help each other understand the mystery that lies at the heart of our existence.

Through spirituality, our religious beliefs are increasingly becoming a part of our lives—rather than *apart* from our lives. While many of us may be more interested than ever in spiritual growth, we may be less firmly planted in traditional religion. Yet, we do want to deepen our relationship to the sacred, to learn from our own as well as from other faith traditions, and to practice in new ways.

SkyLight Paths sees both believers and seekers as a community that increasingly transcends traditional boundaries of religion and denomination—people wanting to learn from each other, *walking together, finding the way.*

For your information and convenience, at the back of this book we have provided a list of other SkyLight Paths books you might find interesting and useful. They cover the following subjects:

Buddhism / Zen	Gnosticism	Mysticism
Catholicism	Hinduism /	Poetry
Children's Books	Vedanta	Prayer
Christianity	Inspiration	Religious Etiquette
Comparative	Islam / Sufism	Retirement
Religion	Judaism / Kabbalah /	Spiritual Biography
Current Events	Enneagram	Spiritual Direction
Earth-Based	Meditation	Spirituality
Spirituality	Midrash Fiction	Women's Interest
Global Spiritual	Monasticism	Worship
Perspectives		

Or phone, fax, mail or e-mail to: SKYLIGHT PATHS Publishing
Sunset Farm Offices, Route 4 • P.O. Box 237 • Woodstock, Vermont 05091
Tel: (802) 457-4000 • Fax: (802) 457-4004 • www.skylightpaths.com
Credit card orders: (800) 962-4544 (8:30AM–5:30PM ET Monday–Friday)
Generous discounts on quantity orders. SATISFACTION GUARANTEED. Prices subject to change.

**For more information about each book,
visit our website at www.skylightpaths.com**